Banner Year

The Championship Season of the 2021-22 Kansas Jayhawks

In the last minute and a half of the 2022 NCAA Championship Game, David McCormack hit two crucial shots that will live forever in the annals of Kansas Basketball history alongside Mario Chalmers' game-tying shot in the 2008 final. The first gave KU the lead by one. Then, after a defensive stop, this jump hook provided the final margin – three – with :22 left to play.

Requests for permission should be addressed to: Ascend Books, LLC, Attn: Rights and Permissions Department, 11722 West 91th Street, Overland Park, KS 66214

First Edition
10 9 8 7 6 5 4 3 2 1

ISBN: print book 979-8-9863584-1-3

Library of Congress Control Number: 2022945040

Publisher: Bob Snodgrass
Editor: Jim Marchiony
Publication Coordinator: Molly Gore
Sales and Marketing: Lenny Cohen
Book Design: Rob Peters

Photo Credits: Photography by Kansas Athletics
Missy Minear, Manager of Photography
Aiden Droge
Chad Cushing

Photos courtesy NCAA: Pages 2-3, Page 120 (top), back cover
Photo courtesy Tarleton State: Page 22
Graphic art for Page 124 created by Brian Gray.

Acknowledgements:
A special thank you to Chris Theisen and Fred Quartlebaum for helping us gather much of our player commentary. They are the best at what they do in their professions and Championship-caliber, just like this team. Our very talented photographer Missy Minear helped us sift through thousands of photos. She did a tremendous job capturing so many amazing moments along this incredible ride. Finally, getting to team up with Jim Marchiony again was a special thrill. He's a legend in our industry and though he'd already given Kansas Athletics 16 of his best years, this project may be his best gift yet. -BH

Publisher's Note: The goal of Ascend Books is to publish quality works. With that goal in mind, we are proud to offer this book to our readers. Please notify the publisher of any erroneous credits or omissions, and corrections will be made to subsequent editions/future printings.

Banner Year is the officially licensed 2021-22 Championship Season Commemorative of the University of Kansas Jayhawks.

Printed in Canada

www.ascendbooks.com

Banner Year

The Championship Season of the 2021-22 Kansas Jayhawks

by Brian Hanni
Foreword by Bill Self
Afterword by David McCormack

Foreword by Bill Self

You could see the emotion from all the players, coaches and staff after our 2022 NCAA title game win over North Carolina. Everyone worked so hard for that common goal, and then we actually did it. What an amazing feeling! We felt elation, but were also overwhelmed and humbled.

It is unbelievable to know that this team will go down in the 124-year history of Kansas basketball as one of its most beloved teams, cherished and remembered by Jayhawk fans across the globe, and to know that we're just a small part of this history. These players came to KU as caretakers of a legacy for this small period. They played here, and they did a remarkable job as caretakers. I don't think our fans, coaching staff, or administration could have asked for anything more than what they have given us.

As their coach, one of the greatest things said to me after the Carolina game was, "Your men played their asses off." And the key word was not "ass" or "off." The key word was "men." A group of guys who weren't mature would have had no chance to win that national

As the clock hit zero I looked to the heavens because I know how much my dad would have appreciated the grit and maturity of this team.

championship unless they played like men. So, I applaud the guys and how they matured into men.

This was a season where there were no issues. None. Everything seemed to be planned by a supreme power, and things fell into place. Sure, we look back and see our loss to Dayton and injuries to key players, but it was the best thing that could have happened for us early in the season. David McCormack's foot was hurt for most of the time, but it let other players develop. Remy Martin was hurt, and though it wasn't the best thing for Remy, it was the best thing for our team. We learned to grind, not expecting him. We knew who we were and then we got the boost we needed. Who would have thought the team that played Kentucky in January would go on to win the national championship? We weren't very good, and they were. Our guys were humbled, but bounced back and asked, "How are we going to get better?" For them to embrace that experience and learn from it is something that coaches dream about.

This team was resilient and aligned with our vision. These men checked all the boxes, every day. They showed up, were fully present, worked, grew, took ownership, were the caretakers and contributors. They had fun, were energized, and added value. Just check our record following these losses: Dayton (8-0), Kentucky (6-1) and TCU (11-0). And in the 11-0 run to

There's no better feeling than talking to your team after a great victory like this. We gave the championship net to David McCormack because although we're all happy that Ochai was named Most Outstanding Player, we know that David could easily have won the award.

the title, this team became the winningest program in college basketball history.

They say that coaches can impact players, but they don't talk enough about how players can impact coaches. What these men did for me, my staff and our Jayhawk family probably wasn't thought out or planned. But when these men knew somebody was not going to be at their best, it was just a natural reaction for them to say, "Hey, we've got to pick up the slack." I'll always be especially close to this team because that is exactly what they did. They propped us up in a way that allowed us to survive, and then allowed us to thrive. I'll never, ever forget that.

I particularly want to say to the 2020 team, guys like Isaiah (Moss), Dot (Devon Dotson), Dok (Udoka Azubuike), and of course Marcus (Garrett): We could have won two of the last three championships. That opportunity was taken away from us by the pandemic. I really believe that was a motivating factor as to why the 2022 team played so well. They were playing for more than just themselves, and that's what teams do. They always put others first. I'm so appreciative of all those guys.

People say we've got good kids. The reason we have good kids isn't because we groomed them after they got to Kansas. The reason we have good kids is because of the people they

The hard work is getting to the Final Four, and that was certainly true for us in the Midwest Regional. I was proud of our guys' toughness and resilience in our great second-half comeback against Miami.

sat and ate dinner with every night while growing up. I personally want to thank all the parents and families of our guys for giving us the opportunity to coach men whose hearts and heads were in the right place.

This book captures the run of the incredible 2021-22 season. It will live on coffee tables and in family rooms. It will be looked at and read often. It will continue to bring back fond memories of an unforgettable team and a Banner Year. It's a must-read book thanks to Brian Hanni's creative telling of the story, David McCormack's afterword, and the incredible work of our photo staff, led by Missy Minear. Enjoy!

Rock Chalk!

Coach Bill Self

One of my favorite moments of the year is listening to the players' speeches on Senior Night. You never know what they're going to say, but you know it's coming straight from the heart.

As I hand the microphone to Mitch Lightfoot on Senior Day it occurs to me how much of a role Mitch has played in our success for what seems like a decade! Little did he know as he took the mic that his commitment to KU was finally going to pay off with the ultimate prize. I think if we hadn't won it he would have figured out a way to play again next year!

Introduction
by Brian Hanni

The 2021-2022 Jayhawks will forever hold a special place in my heart because in realizing their own hoop dreams, they also helped me fulfill my biggest broadcasting aspiration – a dream that dated back further than any of these 'Hawks had even been alive. Getting a front row seat on their journey to a title and having the chance to tell their stories both on-air and now in print, have been some of the greatest privileges of my life.

Every sportscaster dreams of getting the chance to call a National Championship run but only a small percentage of us are lucky enough to ever experience it. We're especially fortunate at Kansas. My predecessor Bob Davis got to call two of them (1988 and 2008), as did Max Falkenstien (1952 and 1988).

How lucky are we to be treated to championship caliber basketball each year at KU? With Bill Self at the helm, Kansas is legitimately in the national title hunt nearly every single season. If you include 2020, when our Jayhawks finished the regular season #1 in the country but the pandemic canceled March Madness, Coach Self has produced ten #1 seeds in the last 16 years. He's had ten 30-win seasons and 16 conference titles in his first 19 years at Kansas. Under Self, KU has become the modern-day model of regular-season dominance and perennial title contention. Thanks to his coaching brilliance and remarkable consistency, every year is a great year at Kansas Basketball. But at a school that only hangs banners

Last second game-winners are always a broadcaster's favorite play to call, especially when they come from an unlikely hero. Against Iowa State at home, everyone (including Dajuan) figured Ochai would take the big shot, but I was so proud to see Harris seize the moment – and the win – when opportunity knocked.

for Final Fours and National Championships, to have a truly "Banner Year," a team must accomplish something very special.

When the expectation is "Final Four or Bust," Banner Years can be quite elusive. Not often do college basketball's best teams over the first four months finish on top in the end. It's just the nature of the toughest postseason format in any American sport. Because of that often-cruel reality, even at a juggernaut like Kansas, you never truly know when your next chance to call a title run might be – or if it will ever come at all. Heartbreaking defeats in 2017 in the Elite 8 in Kansas City and the following year at the Final Four in New Orleans taught me to savor each win along the way. Having those 2020 postseason dreams dashed before even tipping off was another reminder to cherish each round of the Dance and never take anything for granted.

With that in mind, I tried to soak up every big moment along the road to seeing our Jayhawks raise a sixth banner in The Phog – and what a journey it was. From Remy Martin's postseason breakout that had #Remergy and #RemyMarchin' trending on Twitter, to becoming the winningest program of all-time after beating Providence, the early-round action had it all. Then came that dominant 47-15 second half in the Windy City, in which our Jayhawks hit the Hurricanes with a storm of their own to earn the program's 16th Final Four.

Heading to New Orleans as the most underrated last-one-seed-still-standing ever was a bit of a unique feeling. The hype around North Carolina/Duke in Coach K's final season was so huge you would have thought Elvis was coming back to open for The Beatles. All that Tobacco Road hoopla and fanfare was just fine by our Jayhawks, though. It allowed them to fly under the radar even as the highest remaining seed still dancing.

Team chemistry was a big reason why Kansas won it all. Self's squad had it and so did our broadcast crew. In Fort Worth, the most colorful of all color analysts, Greg Gurley (left), joined me, producer/engineer Steve Kincaid and pre- and postgame host Sean Kellerman (far right), as we watched the Jayhawks advance to the Sweet 16.

Ochai Agbaji's scorching hot start versus Villanova not only proved he'd shaken a late-season shooting slump, but it also felt like cathartic redemption for the 3-point barrage that Jay Wright's Wildcats hit us with early in the 2018 matchup. This one wasn't quite 22-4 out of the gates like in San Antonio, but a 16-5 counterpunch felt pretty satisfying four years later in the same round. Ochai and David were both brilliant against Villanova, and it set the stage for us all to realize our dreams on Monday night.

On the eve of that incredible opportunity both on the floor and on the mic, I was wrestling with just what to say in the closing moments should KU win it all. I called the last two announcers to broadcast title wins – Dave Koehn of Virginia and John Morris of Baylor – and asked their advice. Wes Durham, another broadcast hero of mine, was there in New Orleans and offered his input as well. Then the ultimate encouragement came from the pinnacle of our profession, fellow Jayhawk Kevin Harlan, who is as gracious as he is talented and who has both inspired and encouraged me at key junctures in my career. He did again that weekend in NOLA.

The consensus I gathered from my peers was that while most don't want to have a call completely scripted for fear of sounding contrived, it is helpful to at least have an idea in mind of what you'd like to convey should that magical moment unfold.

That's when my mind ventured back to that concept of a truly "Banner Year" at Kansas. I thought about all the tremendous Jayhawk teams and outstanding tourney runs that came up just short of being banner-worthy. I pondered how set-apart teams like 1922, 1923, 1952, 1988 and 2008 are in Kansas lore. You only earn a spot in the rafters on the north side of college basketball's greatest arena if you proved to be the absolute best in a given year. Those are the banner teams that delivered Banner Years, and that was what was at stake on Monday night.

With those two words on the tip of my tongue and hopes as high as Wilt's wingspan was wide, I took the

The only thing better than realizing your dreams, is doing it with people you love. Here's our tight-knit crew again, including long-time pre- and postgame host, David Lawrence (left). David has covered six Final Fours and now two title teams.

air ready to describe what I hoped would wind up being one of the greatest nights in KU's illustrious history. As we all know by now, it certainly didn't start out that way.

Carolina went on a 18-3 run to close out the half and our Jayhawks were down a whopping 15 at the break. I remember my broadcast partner Greg Gurley and I wondering what Coach Self must have been saying in the Kansas locker room on the heels of such a deflating first half. Turns out, not at all surprisingly, the Hall of Famer had just the right words to ignite his team. "Would you rather be down nine with two minutes to play or down 15 with 20 minutes left?" His hypothetical, of course, referenced the last Kansas team to win it all, and unanimously the 2022 Jayhawks preferred their predicament to what the 2008 team had to overcome.

As he was delivering the greatest halftime pep talk of all-time (one that would inspire the largest comeback in title game history), Greg and I were trying to keep hope alive on the Jayhawk Network. I remember saying right before the ball was inbounded to start the second half, "Perhaps tomorrow, next week and for the rest of our lives we'll all reminisce about where we were when Kansas made that epic, historic second-half comeback on college basketball's biggest stage. We'll talk for ages about whatever Bill Self said to light that fire and ignite his team. Maybe, just maybe, that dream is still alive."

When I uttered those words I genuinely believed it could happen, but figured the deficit would have to shrink by a point per minute, and then maybe by the under-4:00 media timeout we'd have ourselves a ballgame. Never in my wildest dreams could I have imagined the Jayhawks would storm back to within one in just 7 minutes and 16 seconds.

That furious comeback and the back-and-forth action that followed down the stretch proved to be the most exciting moments of my career. Thanks to CB's early half heroics, another epic Remy run and then two huge buckets from Big Dave, we all had our dreams come true that night and I got to describe the finishing touches to a truly "Banner Year," just like I'd hoped.

It was all so surreal in the end. Caleb Love's final shot missed, the horn sounded, I belted out my final call, and next came something you could never script: a hug from the All-American. As time expired, an elated Agbaji was looking for a couple familiar faces to celebrate with, and though Greg and mine were made for radio, at least they were ones he recognized. He charged over with high fives and a hug. If you were listening in that moment, you heard me shout, "I love you, brother." "It's a Banner Year for Kansas Basketball," may have been premeditated, but those four words spontaneously came from the heart.

I do love Och and all our Jayhawks who gave us memories in 2022 that we will cherish for a lifetime. I love them for showing a truly unique level of team chemistry, unlike any I've ever been around. That type of selflessness and cohesiveness should be a lesson to young Jayhawk fans on the DNA of a true championship team. I'm grateful for the family atmosphere Coach Self has cultivated in his program and the inclusiveness he offers me and my teammates on the Jayhawk Network. We all got to live out a dream in 2022. I hope you enjoy the pages ahead and the pictures, quotes and poetic storytelling that attempt to capture what wasn't just an incredible year – we get those all the time at Kansas – 2022 was a Banner Year.

Brian Hanni

Gather 'round and hear the tale
Of a Jayhawk team beloved by all.
And their amazing run to a title:
A "Banner Year" for Kansas Basketball.

Sitting on Floor (left to right) — Thomas Boardman (manager), Carson Linnes (manager), David Gunnigle (manager), Justin Dickerson (manager), Patrick Cassidy (manager), Andrew Korta (manager)

Middle Row (left to right) — Bill Cowgill (associate director, sports medicine), Jeremy Case (assistant coach), Norm Roberts (assistant coach), Remy Martin, Jalen Coleman-Lands, Cam Martin, David McCormack, Bill Self (head coach), Mitch Lightfoot, Ochai Agbaji, Chris Teahan, Kurtis Townsend (assistant coach), Fred Quartlebaum (director, basketball operations), Brennan

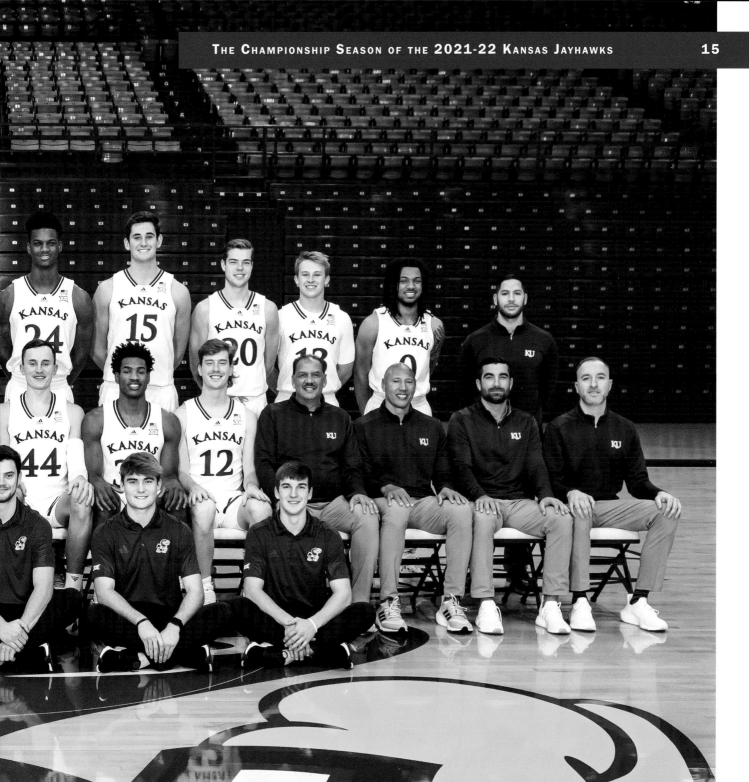

Bechard (director, student-athlete development), Brady Morningstar (video coordinator)
Back Row (left to right) — Samantha Thomas (trainer), Jaden Gard (head manager), Joseph Yesufu, Dajuan Harris Jr., Kyle Cuffe Jr., Christian Braun, Jalen Wilson, Zach Clemence, KJ Adams Jr., Dillon Wilhite, Michael Jankovich, Charlie McCarthy, Bobby Pettiford, Dr. Ramsey Nijem (director, sports performance)

Pure elation! The Jayhawks hoist the 2022 Big 12 Championship trophy after beating Texas in Allen Fieldhouse.

Big 12 Commissioner Bob Bowlsby congratulates Most Outstanding Player Ochai Agbaji and the rest of the victorious Jayhawks after the Big 12 Tournament in Kansas City.

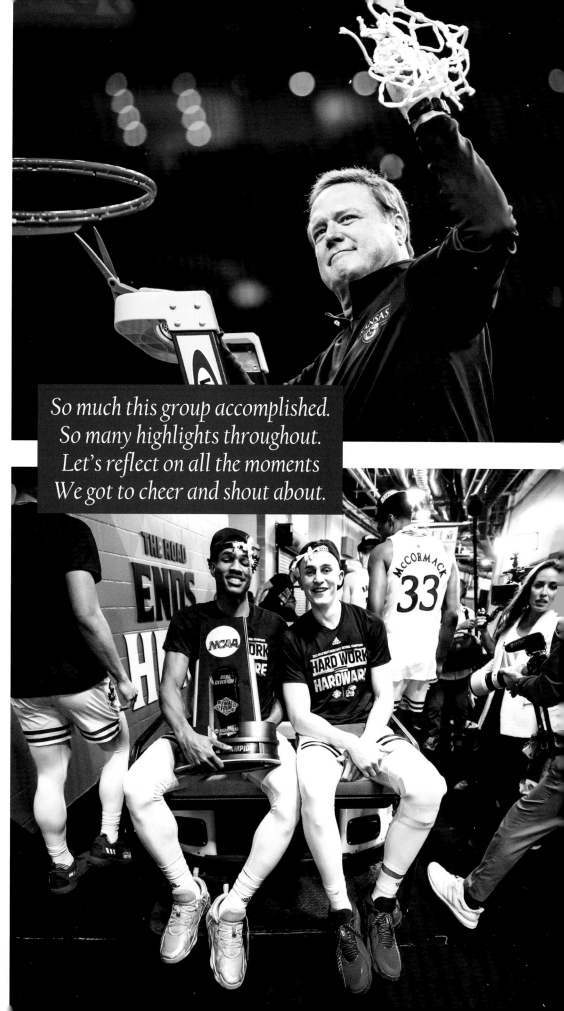

So much this group accomplished.
So many highlights throughout.
Let's reflect on all the moments
We got to cheer and shout about.

(top right) Head Coach Bill Self is one of only two active college coaches (Rick Pitino is the other) to achieve multiple NCAA Championships.

When you're national champions you get to go from the court to the locker room on the back of a golf cart.

Michigan State in NYC
87-74 Kansas

Ochai Agbaji: 29 points (9-17 FG, 3-6 3's, 8-8 FT).
Remy Martin: 15 points (5-9 FG).

It all got started in NYC:
"The City that Never Sleeps."
No pundits were sleeping on Kansas
Because our Jayhawks played for keeps.

I came back for this. To be on this stage and be in this moment. To lead my team to a win. That's why I chose to come back.

— Ochai Agbaji

Mitch Lightfoot dunks during pregame warmups under the iconic roof of Madison Square Garden. ESPN's College GameDay crew prepares at their desk on the court in the background.

A statement was made in the Garden.
That night Ochai made it clear;
His 29 points put the world on notice
That this would be his year.

Ochai has had big games, but I don't know if he's had a bigger game on a bigger stage with the bright lights.
—Bill Self

When Ochai Agbaji wasn't shooting from the outside, he was putting pressure on the Spartan defense and getting fouled. He was 8-for-8 from the line.

Ochai Agbaji gathers David McCormack, Christian Braun and Dajuan Harris Jr. for some strategy. Braun led KU in rebounds (8), and Harris Jr. led the team in assists (4) and steals (3).

New addition Remy Martin
Made quite a Jayhawk debut.
Though quiet in the first half,
In the second he came through.

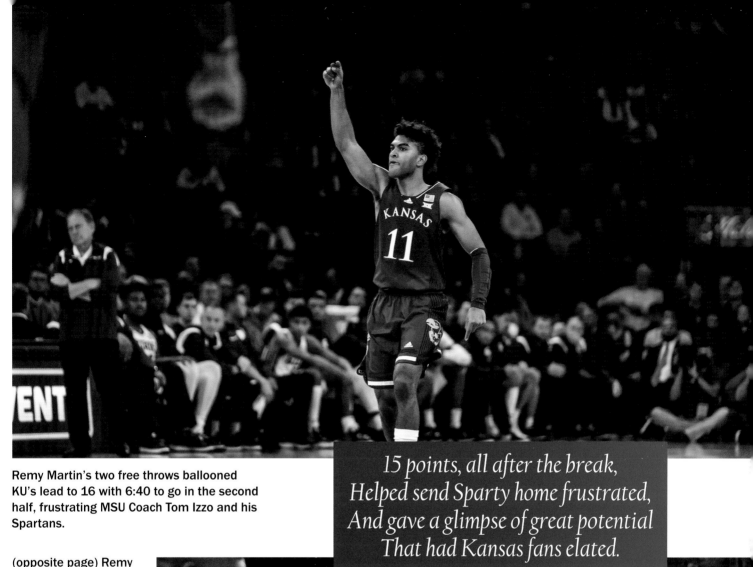

Remy Martin's two free throws ballooned KU's lead to 16 with 6:40 to go in the second half, frustrating MSU Coach Tom Izzo and his Spartans.

(opposite page) Remy Martin drives for two of his 15 points in the Champions Classic against Michigan State in Madison Square Garden.

15 points, all after the break,
Helped send Sparty home frustrated,
And gave a glimpse of great potential
That had Kansas fans elated.

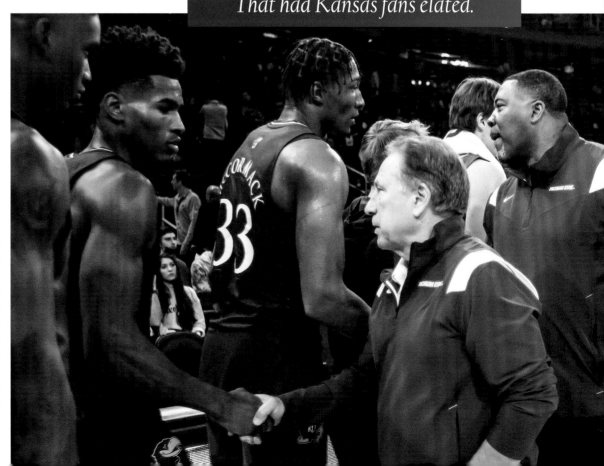

Spartan Coach Tom Izzo shakes hands with Ochai Agbaji after KU's victory. Izzo is one of five Hall-of-Fame coaches that Bill Self and the Jayhawks faced in 2021-22. Jay Wright, Rick Pitino, John Calipari and Bob Huggins (three times) complete the list.

Tarleton State
88-62 Kansas

Ochai Agbaji: 25 points (11-16 FG). McCormack, Braun: Five blocks each.

The Jayhawks' home opener is always a special event; the large American flag added even more impact to the pregame festivities.

> Then it was back home to the Fieldhouse,
> To face a foe long ago befriended.
> Two old buddies went toe-to-toe
> As an astounding home streak extended.

The friendship between Tarleton State Coach Billy Gillispie and KU Coach Bill Self goes back decades. Gillispie served as an assistant coach on Self's teams at Tulsa and Illinois.

49 straight home-opening wins,
Dating back to 1973.
Coaches Owens, Brown, Williams and Self,
All had a hand in that history.

David McCormack emphatically denies Javontae Hopkins' layup attempt in the first half of KU's home-opening victory over Tarleton State. McCormack and Christian Braun each had five blocks and eight rebounds.

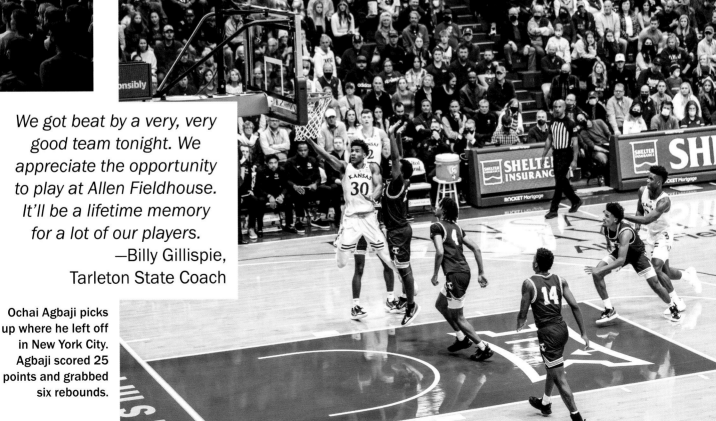

We got beat by a very, very good team tonight. We appreciate the opportunity to play at Allen Fieldhouse. It'll be a lifetime memory for a lot of our players.
—Billy Gillispie,
Tarleton State Coach

Ochai Agbaji picks up where he left off in New York City. Agbaji scored 25 points and grabbed six rebounds.

Stony Brook
88-59 Kansas

Ochai Agbaji: 25 points (10-19 FG).

KU then dispatched of Stony Brook,
And went to Disney 3-0.

Ochai Agbaji continued to flash his All-America form, registering 25 points, three assists and two steals. The Jayhawks broke the game wide open with a 14-0 second-half run.

Stony Brook's Anthony Roberts has nowhere to go, hounded by Ochai Agbaji and Joseph Yesufu. The Jayhawks harassed the Seawolves into 14 turnovers and 37.5% shooting from the field.

North Texas in Orlando

71-59 Kansas

Ochai Agbaji: 18 points (6-12 FG). Christian Braun: 16 points (6-8 FG).

Facing a team from his home town (Denton, Texas), Jalen Wilson connected on three of his four field-goal attempts and contributed five rebounds and four assists to the Jayhawk victory.

But after knocking off North Texas, It was the Flyers who stole the show...

Jalen Coleman-Lands drives past a double-team during KU's victory over North Texas. The Jayhawks led by as many as 20 in the second half in the opener of the ESPN Events Invitational.

Dayton in Orlando
74-73 Dayton

Ochai Agbaji: 21 points (8-16 FG). Christian Braun: 17 points (8-12 FG).
Remy Martin: 17 points (7-11 FG).

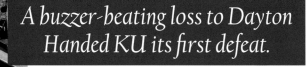

A buzzer-beating loss to Dayton Handed KU its first defeat.

Christian Braun soars above Dayton's Koby Brea for two of his 17 points. Braun added four steals and a team-high five assists, while Ochai Agbaji scored over 20 points for the fourth time in the season's first five games.

The bottom line is, we didn't execute when we needed to. It was a heck of a shot. They deserved it. It was a great basketball game.
— Bill Self

Despite the lunging effort of Christian Braun, Dayton's Mustapha Amzil launches a buzzer-beater that danced on the rim, glanced off the glass and dropped, giving the Flyers a one-point victory.

Iona in Orlando
96-83 Kansas

Christian Braun: 18 pts (8-15 FG). Ochai Agbaji: 17 points (8-14 FG).

But Self rallied his troops to beat Pitino, Getting the 'Hawks back on their feet.

"Now that I've faced Kansas, I'm glad we didn't play them in all those years. I've always admired Bill Self. I've always thought he's one of the best coaches in the game. What I admire most is, whether it's his fast break, offensive sets or rebounding, he doesn't have a weakness as a coach."
—Iona Coach Rick Pitino

Remy Martin passes around the Iona defense to a waiting David McCormack. Martin dished a team-high five assists to complement his 11 points and five rebounds.

Hall-of-Fame Coach Rick Pitino and Hall-of-Famer Bill Self congratulate one another after the Jayhawks beat Iona. It was KU's second of seven matchups against HOF coaches in 2021-22.

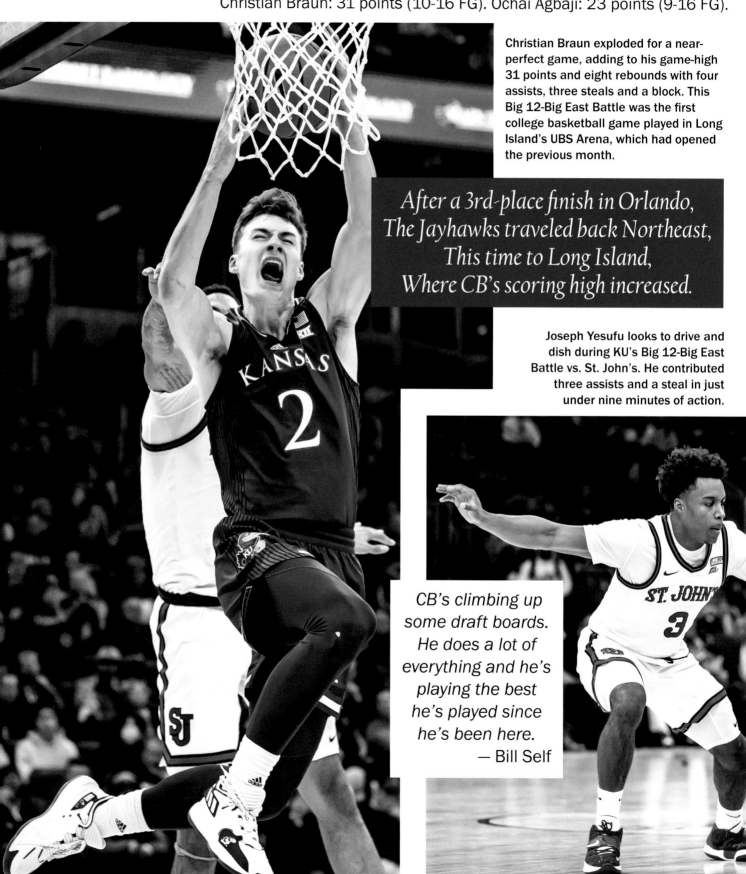

at St. John's
95-75 Kansas

Christian Braun: 31 points (10-16 FG). Ochai Agbaji: 23 points (9-16 FG).

Christian Braun exploded for a near-perfect game, adding to his game-high 31 points and eight rebounds with four assists, three steals and a block. This Big 12-Big East Battle was the first college basketball game played in Long Island's UBS Arena, which had opened the previous month.

After a 3rd-place finish in Orlando,
The Jayhawks traveled back Northeast,
This time to Long Island,
Where CB's scoring high increased.

Joseph Yesufu looks to drive and dish during KU's Big 12-Big East Battle vs. St. John's. He contributed three assists and a steal in just under nine minutes of action.

CB's climbing up some draft boards. He does a lot of everything and he's playing the best he's played since he's been here.
— Bill Self

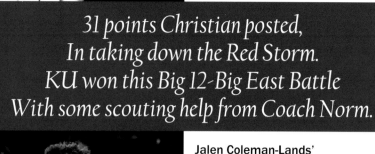

*31 points Christian posted,
In taking down the Red Storm.
KU won this Big 12-Big East Battle
With some scouting help from Coach Norm.*

Jalen Coleman-Lands'
three-point field goal
in the second half
gave the Jayhawks a
20-point lead.

I think any time you show personality it's important. Energy's contagious and I think CB's much better when he's showing he's enjoying being out there.
— Bill Self

This was a homecoming for KU
Assistant Coach Norm Roberts, who
coached St. John's from 2004-2010.
Roberts (left, next to Assistant Coach
Kurtis Townsend) looks over the
scouting report for this game.

UTEP
78-52 Kansas

Ochai Agbaji: 23 points (9-12 FG). Christian Braun: 20 points (9-13 FG).

Ochai Agbaji's dunk put the Jayhawks ahead by 23 in the first half. KU shot 59% from the field in the first half en route to a 42-21 halftime lead.

Christian Braun connects on his only three of the game, with an assist from Ochai Agbaji.

Obviously, those two carried us tonight. They're playing at a pretty high level.
— Bill Self on Agbaji and Braun

"Kansas City here we come,"
KU's annual trip to KC, MO.
And two local kids led the way,
Putting on a stellar shooting show.

KANSAS 18:17 > UTEP

In blowing out the Miners,
Och and CB combined for 43.
And their 18 of 25 shooting
Was quite the sight to see.

Christian Braun gets the Jayhawks going against UTEP in T-Mobile Center in Kansas City. He had six rebounds and a steal to go along with his 20 points.

We don't need to be surprised anymore or think it's some little run he's on. That's Ochai. That's who he is.
—Christian Braun on Agbaji

Ochai Agbaji thanks a teammate for a good pass. UTEP marked the sixth time in eight games this season he scored more than 20 points.

Missouri
102-65 Kansas

Ochai Agbaji: 21 points (7-12 FG, 5-7 3's). Dajuan Harris: 13 pts (5-6 FG).

The north-end student section is amped for the renewal of the Border Showdown in Allen Fieldhouse. Missouri hadn't played in the Fieldhouse since Feb. 25, 2012.

The student section in the south end of the Fieldhouse does its part, too, by distracting DaJuan Gordon at the foul line. It worked. Gordon missed two of his three free throws on the afternoon.

This game means a lot to a lot of people, so I wanted to come out and show it. That was the most fun I've had in my life. I think I was born for that.
—Christian Braun

Then after nearly a decade, The Border rivalry was restored. And so too was KU's dominance, 102 points our Jayhawks scored!

Christian Braun wipes out Yaya Keita's layup attempt, one of Braun's three blocks against Missouri. He also had four rebounds and three assists.

Christian Braun brings the house down with a fast-break dunk off a Remy Martin assist. Braun finished with 13 points on five-of-nine shooting from the field.

(right) Dajuan Harris Jr. drives toward the lane in the first half against Missouri. He added two rebounds, two assists and a steal to his stellar shooting performance.

Remy Martin contributed 10 points, five assists and three rebounds to KU's largest margin of victory over Missouri in 44 years, and the third-largest margin of victory in the 270-game history of the series.

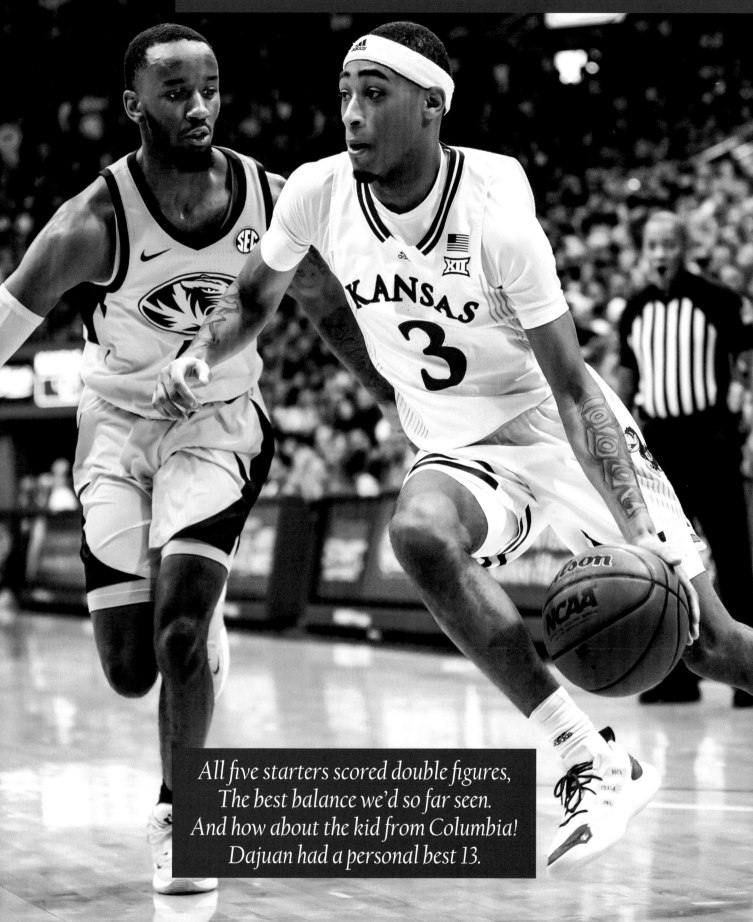

All five starters scored double figures,
The best balance we'd so far seen.
And how about the kid from Columbia!
Dajuan had a personal best 13.

Stephen F. Austin
80-72 Kansas

Christian Braun: 21 points (8-12 FG), six rebounds.

Christian Braun dives to tie up SFA's former Jayhawk Latrell Jossell. In addition to his team-leading 21 points, Braun had six rebounds, three assists, two blocks and a steal.

With some direction from Coach Self, Remy Martin scored 15 points, had four assists and two steals.

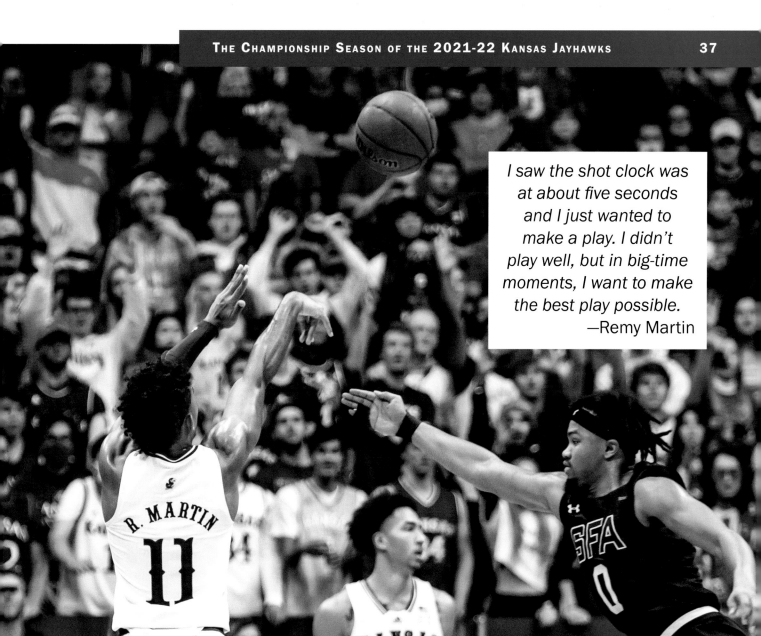

I saw the shot clock was at about five seconds and I just wanted to make a play. I didn't play well, but in big-time moments, I want to make the best play possible.
—Remy Martin

Remy Martin's three-pointer with 35 seconds left gives KU a six-point lead and some much-needed breathing room.

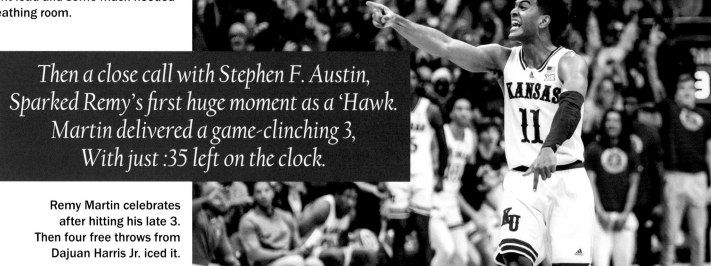

Then a close call with Stephen F. Austin,
Sparked Remy's first huge moment as a 'Hawk.
Martin delivered a game-clinching 3,
With just :35 left on the clock.

Remy Martin celebrates after hitting his late 3. Then four free throws from Dajuan Harris Jr. iced it.

Nevada
88-61 Kansas
Christian Braun: 22 points (8-14 FG).

After a home win over Nevada,
The Jayhawks celebrated New Year's Day...

Mitch Lightfoot's dunk, off a Dajuan Harris Jr. assist, extends the Jayhawks' first-half lead to 10 points. Harris Jr. registered a game-high five assists to complement his 14 points.

Christian Braun drives to the hoop in search of two of his game-high 22 points. He did it all against Nevada, including four rebounds, two assists, two steals and two blocks.

George Mason
76-67 Kansas

Jalen Coleman-Lands: 20 points (7-9 FG, 5-7 3's). Mitch Lightfoot 14 points (7-7 FG).

With a victory over George Mason,
In which J-Cole led the way.

Jalen Coleman-Lands drives past George Mason's DeVon Cooper. Coleman-Lands added three assists and two steals to his game-high 20 points in a very productive 24 minutes of action.

With KU's starters shooting a combined 12-for-44, Jalen Coleman-Lands came to the rescue. Here he follows through on one of his five 3-pointers.

Jalen wasn't the only senior Starting the year off on the right foot. The Jayhawks got a perfect shooting line, 7-for-7 from Mitch Lightfoot.

Mitch Lightfoot was perfect from the field, including this second-half dunk, helping the KU bench outscore the George Mason bench, 38-3.

Our starters were terrific against Nevada and probably that poor today. And our bench was awful against Nevada and were probably even better than that today. We wouldn't have won the game without Coleman-Lands or Lightfoot; they gave us a chance to win.
—Bill Self

Christian Braun elevates to block the shot of George Mason's Xavier Johnson, while KJ Adams Jr. offers support.

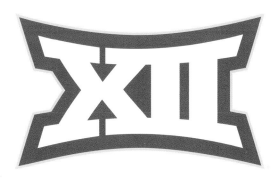

BIG 12 CONFERENCE

Then it was off to Stillwater,
To tip off the Big 12 slate.
Could the Jayhawks corral the Cowboys
For a huge win out the gate?

The Jayhawks huddle up at practice in historic Gallagher-Iba Arena as they begin their quest for Coach Self's 16th Big 12 Conference title in his 19th year at Kansas.

at Oklahoma State
74-63 Kansas

David McCormack: 17 points (7-13 FG), 15 rebounds.

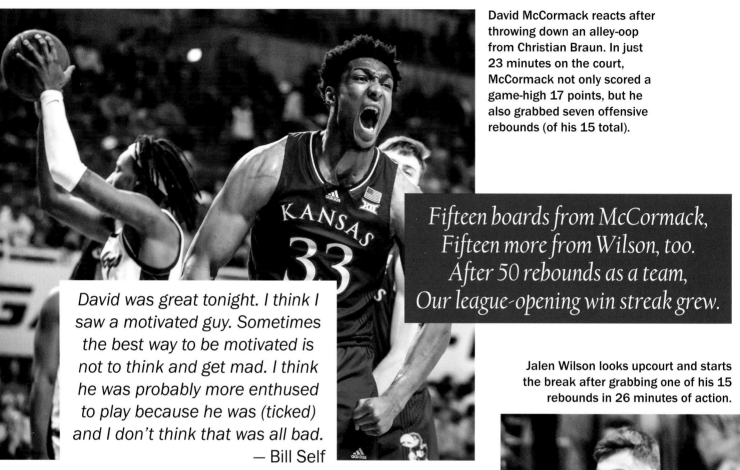

David McCormack reacts after throwing down an alley-oop from Christian Braun. In just 23 minutes on the court, McCormack not only scored a game-high 17 points, but he also grabbed seven offensive rebounds (of his 15 total).

Fifteen boards from McCormack,
Fifteen more from Wilson, too.
After 50 rebounds as a team,
Our league-opening win streak grew.

David was great tonight. I think I saw a motivated guy. Sometimes the best way to be motivated is not to think and get mad. I think he was probably more enthused to play because he was (ticked) and I don't think that was all bad.
— Bill Self

Jalen Wilson looks upcourt and starts the break after grabbing one of his 15 rebounds in 26 minutes of action.

To win a game on the road and miss 19 straight shots, that's not going to happen very often.
—Bill Self

Christian Braun goes up and under OSU's Moussa Cisse for two of his 15 points. Braun added six rebounds and six assists to the effort.

For an incredible 31st consecutive year, KU won its first conference game. 12 by Coach Williams, 19 by Self, Both in the Hall of Fame.

Although it's nice to be back home, it's never easy for Coach Bill Self when KU plays at his alma mater. On this night his Jayhawks surged ahead early by 14, then missed 19 straight shots over a span of nearly 10 minutes, then went on a 21-7 run to take control.

at Texas Tech
75-67 Texas Tech

Ochai Agbaji: 24 points (7-12 FG, 6-9 3's). Jalen Wilson: 20 points (6-8 FG).

Jalen Wilson starts his drive against Tech's Clarence Nadolny. Wilson scored 20, but Tech outscored KU 44-18 in the paint and led virtually the entire game.

Iowa State
62-61 Kansas

Ochai Agbaji: 22 points (8-15 FG, 4-8 3's), seven rebounds. Dajuan Harris Jr.: 12 points.

After a tough road loss in Lubbock, The Cyclones did all they could to scare us.

KJ Adams Jr. comes out of the gate quickly in his only start of the season, slamming down KU's first field goal of the game off an assist from Jalen Wilson.

I haven't hit a game-winner in so long. I thought Ochai was going to take the last shot, but when he started dribbling my way it opened a little crease for me and I heard Coach say, "Get in the lane," so I just drove it and made a play.
—Dajuan Harris Jr.

Dajuan Harris Jr. drives through and over three Iowa State Cyclones to lay in the game-winner in the game's waning seconds. It marked the fourth and final lead change in the final 36 seconds.

The Jayhawks celebrate a true nailbiter in Allen Fieldhouse. How tense was it? Both teams had leads of nine, and the lead changed hands nine times. The Cyclones led for more than 18 minutes, KU for 20.

But the 'Hawks won at the buzzer, Thanks to a driving flip by Harris.

West Virginia
85-59 Kansas

Jalen Wilson: 23 points (10-13 FG), eight rebounds.
David McCormack: 19 points (9-13 FG), 15 rebounds (10 offensive).

They were both great. Jalen was fabulous in just about every area, and David, that was probably as dominant as he's played this year.

— Bill Self

David McCormack emphatically throws down two of his 19 points. He also contributed three assists and a block, and 10 of his game-high 15 rebounds were on the offensive end.

An appreciative Allen Fieldhouse crowd honors Warren Corman at halftime of the West Virginia game Jan. 15. Corman, 95, is the lone surviving member of the team of architects that designed Allen Fieldhouse in the 1950's. He and his wife, Mary, are standing next to a copy of the original front page of the building's blueprint, which is now displayed in the Booth Family Hall of Athletics.

*A home rout of West Virginia
Kept Huggy winless in the Phog.
And Jalen Wilson then got rolling,
A career-high 23 he logged.*

Jalen Wilson's dunk, two of his 16 second-half points, helped KU turn a two-point halftime lead into a rout. Wilson also dished out five assists and had two steals.

Jalen Wilson celebrates after his 3-pointer, assisted by Christian Braun, extends the Jayhawk lead to 20. Wilson went 3-of-6 from beyond the arc.

at Oklahoma
67-64 Kansas

Jalen Wilson: 16 points (6-10 FG), 8 rebounds. Christian Braun: 15 points (5-8 FG, 3-5 3's).

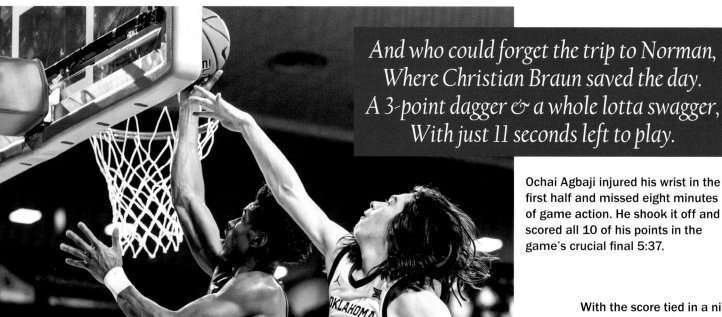

And who could forget the trip to Norman,
Where Christian Braun saved the day.
A 3-point dagger & a whole lotta swagger,
With just 11 seconds left to play.

Ochai Agbaji injured his wrist in the first half and missed eight minutes of game action. He shook it off and scored all 10 of his points in the game's crucial final 5:37.

With the score tied in a nip-and-tuck battle, Christian Braun launches a 3-pointer that swishes with 11 seconds left in the game to put KU ahead for good.

Ochai has been our best player all year long and CB's been our second best, so for those guys to step up and make those plays in the last four minutes speaks volumes of talent, but also toughness and character.
— Bill Self

Christian Braun had been hearing it all night from the OU fans in the courtside seats. He answered with a clutch three – and some words of his own.

Christian Braun celebrates in the locker room with his happy teammates. The victory made KU 4-1 or better in Big 12 play for the 16th consecutive season.

at Kansas State
78-75 Kansas

Ochai Agbaji: 29 points (10-18 FG), seven rebounds.
David McCormack: 11 points, 15 rebounds (eight offensive).

*Then with heavy hearts,
Our 'Hawks traveled to play K-State.*

*Driven to win this one for their Coach,
The Jayhawks came back late.*

Christian Braun enters the court for pregame warmups in front of a full-throated Kansas State student section.

(opposite page) All eyes and ears were on Coach Self, who was coaching with a heavy heart after the passing of his father, Bill Self Sr., earlier in the week.

The Jayhawks wore pregame shooting shirts that honored LaVannes Squires, who in 1951 became the first African-American to play for KU. The Wildcats wore similar shirts to honor Gene Wilson, who broke the color barrier at KSU the same season.

To win this one like that was something extra because the way we won it was exactly the way my dad lived: grind it out and make the most of every situation. So that means something to me. He would have respected how hard the kids tried. That would have been special to him.

— Bill Self

With just over 11 seconds to go and KU down one, Ochai Agbaji starts his drive to the basket.

Ochai Agbaji knifes in between two Wildcats and hits the game-winner with :09 remaining in the game, continuing KU's recent string of late-game heroics. It was KU's first lead since taking a brief 7-5 lead two-and-a-half minutes into the game.

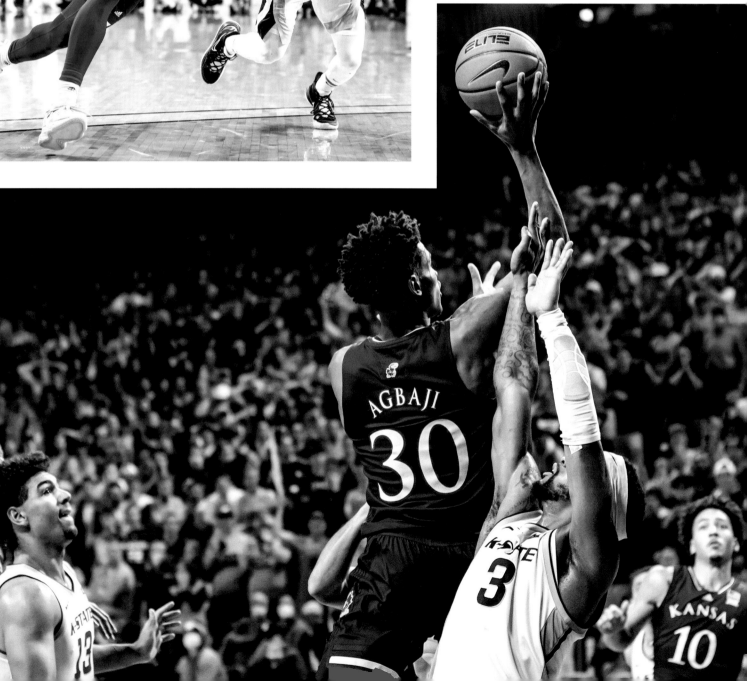

Jalen Wilson revels in the jeers from the Kansas State fans after his 16-point, 10-rebound performance in Manhattan.

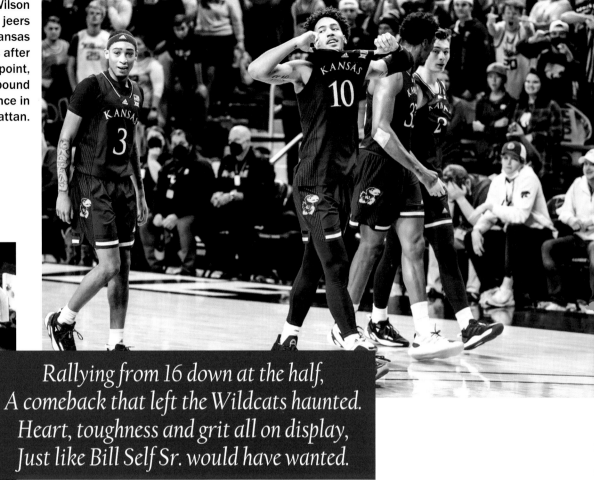

Rallying from 16 down at the half,
A comeback that left the Wildcats haunted.
Heart, toughness and grit all on display,
Just like Bill Self Sr. would have wanted.

Coach Self and the team celebrate in the locker room after overcoming the largest halftime deficit (16) in a victory in KU history.

Texas Tech
94-91 (2OT) Kansas

Ochai Agbaji: 37 points (13-23 FG, 7-12 3's).

Ochai Agbaji gets by fellow first-team All-Big 12 forward Bryson Williams. Agbaji and Williams put on a show for the Allen Fieldhouse crowd, combining for 70 points (27 for 42 from the field).

It's too early to give out accolades. We know that, and Ochai knows that, but that's the best player in the country right now to date. And no one can say they've made more clutch plays than what he has for us this year.
—Bill Self

Next came the thriller with Texas Tech,
A game that took two overtimes to decide.

David McCormack contributed 13 points and five rebounds to the Jayhawks' victory. This was a battle in the paint all night: Texas Tech scored 46 points there, the Jayhawks 40.

Christian Braun and Ochai Agbaji embrace in the locker room after KU's emotional victory in Allen Fieldhouse. Braun had quite the game as well: 15 points, seven rebounds and six assists.

Ochai Agbaji, off a dish from Dajuan Harris Jr., hits an epic 3 over the outstretched arms of future Jayhawk Kevin McCullar and Daniel Batcho to tie the game with seven-tenths of a second left and send it to a second overtime as KU's recent run of late-game magic continued.

KU got 37 more from Ochai,
Whose clutch OT 3 helped turn the tide.

Kentucky
80-62 Kentucky
Christian Braun: 13 points (5-11 FG).

Then in a home loss to Kentucky,
The Jayhawks took it on the chin.
But they'd race past those Wildcats later,
In the chase for all-time wins.

ESPN's College GameDay originated from Allen Fieldhouse the morning of the Kentucky game, marking the 10th time that the Fieldhouse has hosted the show. (From left) Rece Davis, LaPhonso Ellis, Seth Greenberg and Jay Bilas did the honors.

Big Jay and the KU students made sure that a raucous atmosphere greeted the ESPN telecast.

Bill Self and Kentucky Coach John Calipari, two former KU graduate assistant coaches and now Hall of Famers, greet each other before the game.

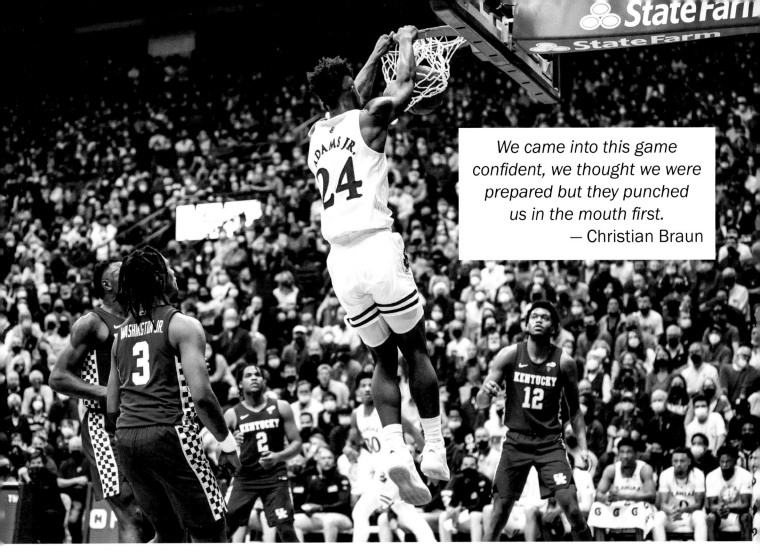

KJ Adams Jr. converts an alley-oop pass from Dajuan Harris Jr. to try to spark a KU rally.

Kentucky's defense stayed mindful of Ochai Agbaji for 40 minutes, holding him to just four field goals. On the other end, Kentucky scored 17 second-chance points off 12 offensive rebounds.

at Iowa State
70-61 Kansas

David McCormack: 14 points (7-7 FG), 14 rebounds.
Dajuan Harris Jr.: 14 points (6-8 FG), eight assists, four steals.

Just play hard. That's my biggest thing. Play hard and everything else will work out. This was a huge confidence boost for me for the future.
—Joseph Yesufu

David McCormack posterizes Robert Jones. McCormack dominated on both ends – aside from his points and rebounds he was perfect from the floor and blocked two shots.

Playing just 29 miles down the road from where he starred at Drake, Joseph Yesufu grabs the ball before former Jayhawk Tristan Enaruna can get it. Yesufu's all-around game included seven points, five rebounds, four assists and three steals, all within 23 minutes of play.

Depth was tested at Iowa State,
As KU played without Och.
But Lil' Joe, Big Dave and 'Juan made sure
That a road win still was poached.

Dajuan Harris Jr. did it all for the Jayhawks in 38 minutes of action in Ames. Here he slips by George Conditt for two of his career-high 14 points.

Coach Bill Self congratulates David McCormack as the Jayhawks gather in KU's happy locker room to celebrate a solid road victory over a 16-5 team.

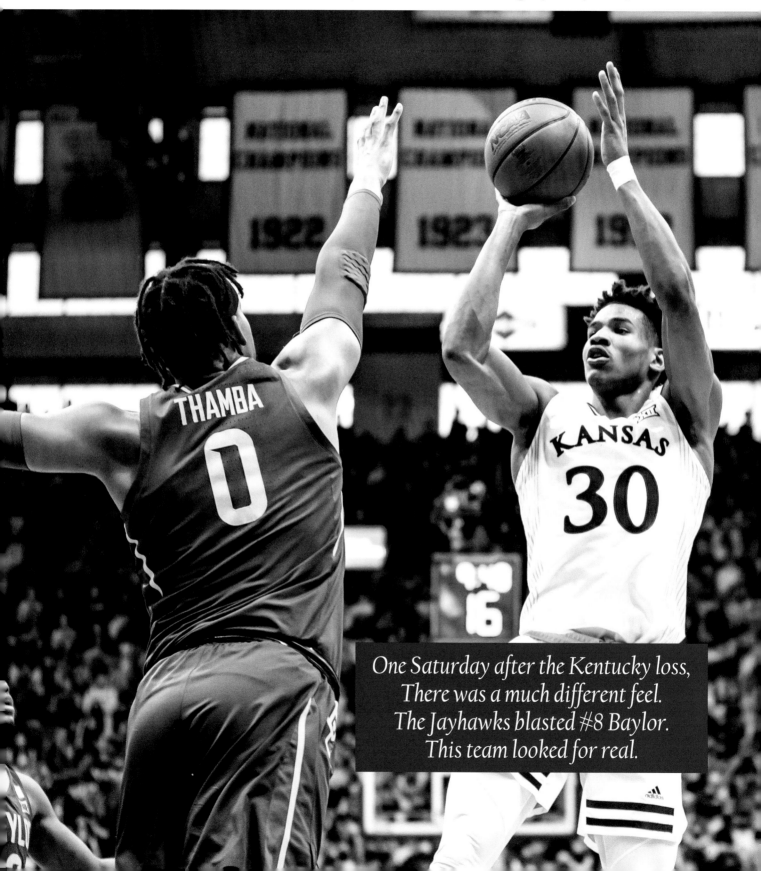

Baylor
83-59 Kansas

Christian Braun: 18 points (8-14 FG), 10 rebounds. Ochai Agbaji: 18 points, nine rebounds.

One Saturday after the Kentucky loss,
There was a much different feel.
The Jayhawks blasted #8 Baylor.
This team looked for real.

Jalen Wilson drives and dishes to Dajuan Harris Jr. Wilson scored 15 on 7-of-10 from the field with seven rebounds, four assists, two steals and a block.

(opposite page) By the time Ochai Agbaji launched this jumper some 10 minutes into the game, KU already led by 15.

The Baylor defense tried all game to hold Ochai Agbaji down. The Bears fouled him five times, and Ochai hit six of his seven free throws.

In front of our fans to lose like we did a week ago to Kentucky, that's not something that we are used to and not something that we're going to get used to either. We knew there was no option but to come in here and play really hard and get one back for the fans. And that's what we did."
— Christian Braun

Ever the emotional catalyst, Christian Braun reacts after converting on his own offensive rebound. His ensuing and-1 free throw gave KU a 20-point lead with 4:15 to go in the first half.

Life is good when your team shoots 27-of-42 from inside the arc (including 48 points in the paint) and you hold your opponent to under 30% from the field. Jalen Wilson did his part by hitting all six of his attempts from two-point range.

The Jayhawks' 34-point lead with about four minutes remaining allowed for some extended time for KU's bench. Michael Jankovich (below left) takes advantage, launching one from three, and Chris Teahan (below right) works the ball around the perimeter.

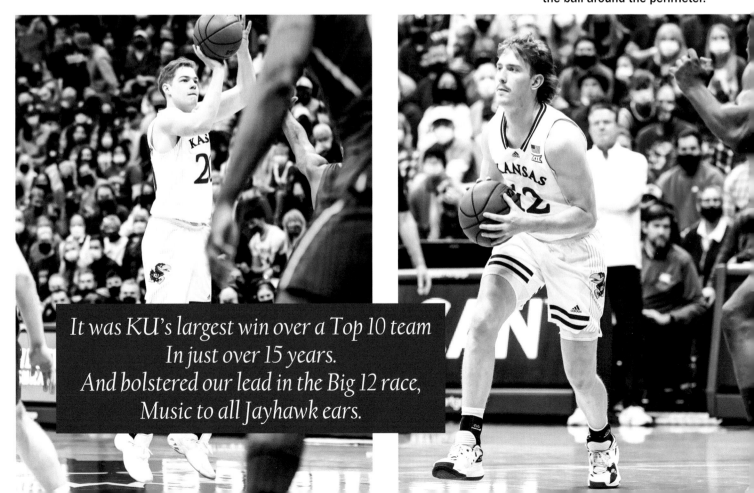

It was KU's largest win over a Top 10 team
In just over 15 years.
And bolstered our lead in the Big 12 race,
Music to all Jayhawk ears.

Texas
79-76 Texas
Jalen Wilson: 18 points (6-10 FG), 11 rebounds.

Jalen Wilson drives for two of his team-high 18 points. His 11 rebounds led both teams. KU shot 58% from the field but committed 15 turnovers and surrendered 13 second-chance points.

After a hard road loss at Texas, Keyed by a tough-luck banked-in three,

Texas' Tre Mitchell contests Ochai Agbaji's path to the rim. Later, Mitchell delivered the game's most impactful moment, a banked-in 3 with 55 seconds remaining that swung momentum Texas' way.

Oklahoma
71-69 Kansas

Jalen Wilson: 22 points (8-12 FG), nine rebounds.
Christian Braun: 18 points (6-10 FG), eight rebounds.

Jalen Wilson scored 14 points in the final 16:08 to help KU overcome a seven-point second-half deficit.

KJ Adams Jr. stretches to alter Jordan Goldwire's attempt to tie the game in the final seconds. KJ had emerged as the Jayhawks' stopper off the bench.

The 'Hawks edged the Sooners at home, Sealed by KJ's play on D.

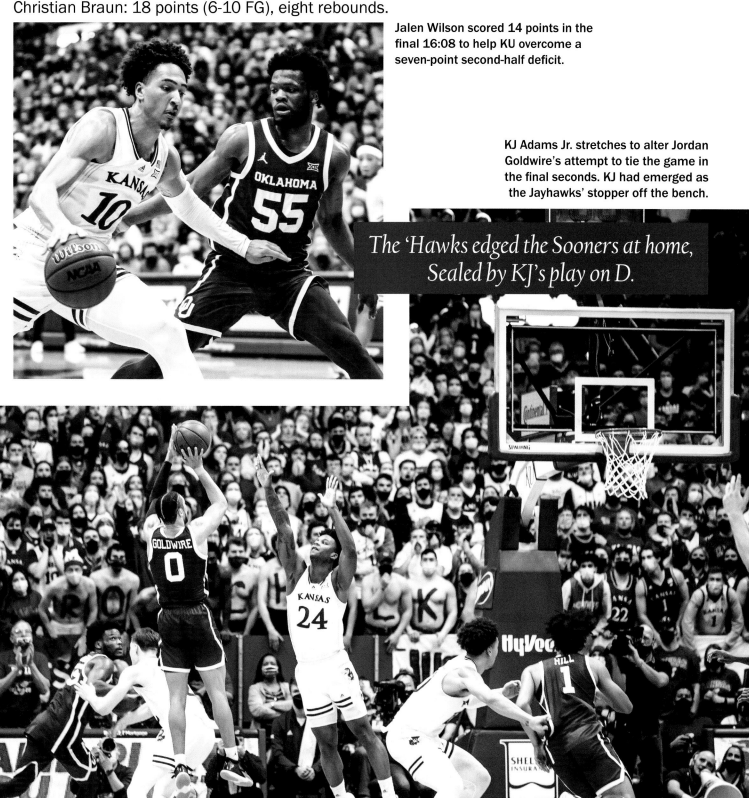

Christian Braun secures the final rebound (his eighth) as time expired to allow KU to escape with the victory.

(below) Zach Clemence grabs a key defensive rebound with 1:22 remaining in the second half and KU up by eight. One minute later the Sooners had cut that lead to one. Jalen Wilson then hit one of two free throws, setting up the final sequence.

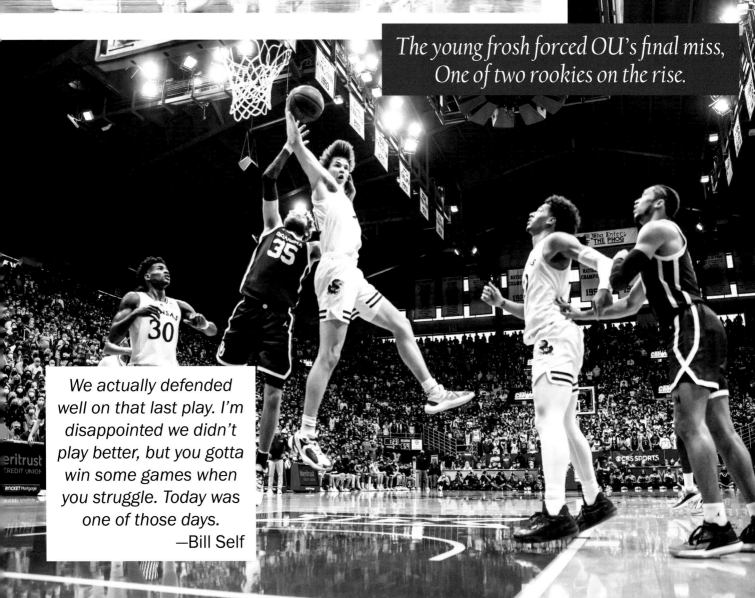

*The young frosh forced OU's final miss,
One of two rookies on the rise.*

We actually defended well on that last play. I'm disappointed we didn't play better, but you gotta win some games when you struggle. Today was one of those days.
—Bill Self

*Zach Clemence returned to provide a spark,
And opened lots of eyes.*

Ochai Agbaji and Dajuan Harris Jr. congratulate Zach Clemence after the freshman's key rebound. Clemence played a significant role earlier as well, hitting a huge 3 with 7:01 to play to give KU the lead for good.

Prior to the game, the Allen Fieldhouse crowd honored Jonathan Phog Bemberger, known as "JP" by his Kansas teammates, on Team IMPACT Day at KU. Team IMPACT's unique multi-year program signs children facing serious illness and disabilities onto collegiate athletics teams across the country. JP's been a part of the KU team for the last two years.

Oklahoma State
76-62 Kansas

Ochai Agbaji: 20 points, seven rebounds. David McCormack: 12 points, 12 rebounds.

Valentine's Day in Allen Fieldhouse brings out the best in Jayhawk fans – and in Baby Jay!

Dajuan Harris Jr. not only scored 12 points on 5-of-9 shooting, but he also contributed a game-high five assists. The Jayhawks were sporting their 1922 Centennial Reverse Retro uniform, honoring KU's 1922 Helms Foundation National Champions.

(opposite page) Ochai Agbaji converts on a fast break after an Oklahoma State turnover to push KU's lead to 22 with 12:59 to go in the game.

Then came a Valentine's victory.
Coach Self's first love is who we beat.
With all five starters in double-figures,
This Jayhawk win was extra sweet.

There's value in winning comfortably. When we won it all in '08, Billy Tubbs told me, 'You don't want to play too many close games. It's exhausting.' If that's a formula for success – not playing close games – then we haven't been very good at that because we've played a ton of them. It was nice to not have to sweat a close game tonight.
— Bill Self

at West Virginia
71-58 Kansas

Ochai Agbaji: 23 points (8-15 FG).
David McCormack: 19 points, 11 rebounds. Jalen Wilson: 10 points, 11 rebounds.

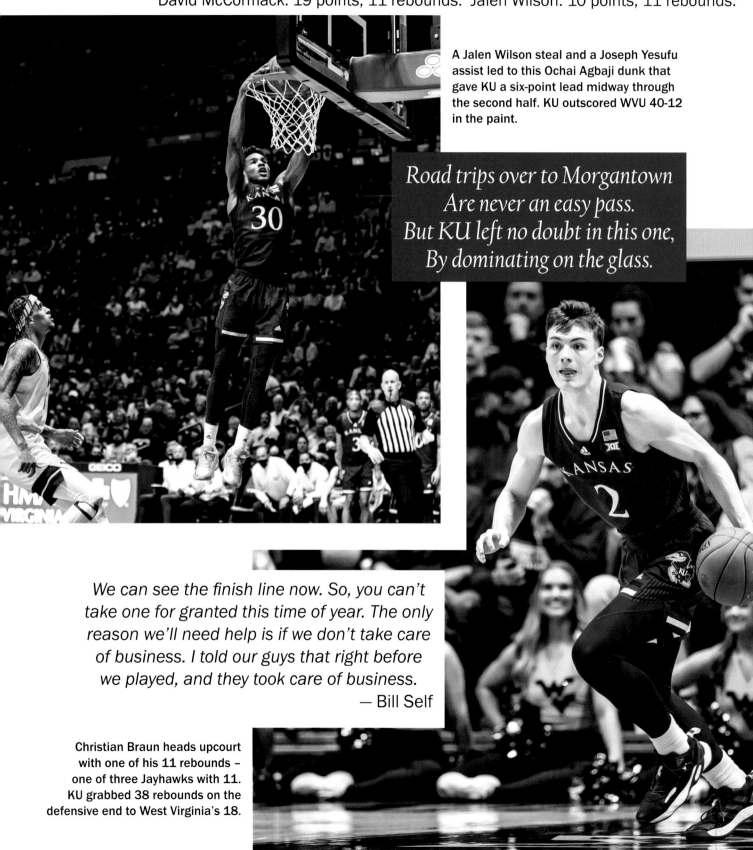

A Jalen Wilson steal and a Joseph Yesufu assist led to this Ochai Agbaji dunk that gave KU a six-point lead midway through the second half. KU outscored WVU 40-12 in the paint.

Road trips over to Morgantown
Are never an easy pass.
But KU left no doubt in this one,
By dominating on the glass.

We can see the finish line now. So, you can't take one for granted this time of year. The only reason we'll need help is if we don't take care of business. I told our guys that right before we played, and they took care of business.
— Bill Self

Christian Braun heads upcourt with one of his 11 rebounds – one of three Jayhawks with 11. KU grabbed 38 rebounds on the defensive end to West Virginia's 18.

Jalen Wilson heads down the lane in the first half at West Virginia. He drew five fouls, hit eight of nine free throws and grabbed 11 rebounds to help keep the Mountaineers at bay.

(below right) David McCormack shows off his hook-shot form that he would put to good use later in the Final Four. The Jayhawks earned a season sweep of the Mountaineers and their coach, Bob Huggins, a 2022 inductee into the Basketball Hall of Fame.

A season sweep of the Mountaineers,
Who we out-boarded by 15!
With 11 each, David, Christian and Jalen
Formed a rebounding machine.

Kansas State
102-83 Kansas

Ochai Agbaji: 23 points (9-13 FG, 4-6 3's). Christian Braun: 20 points (8-12 FG)

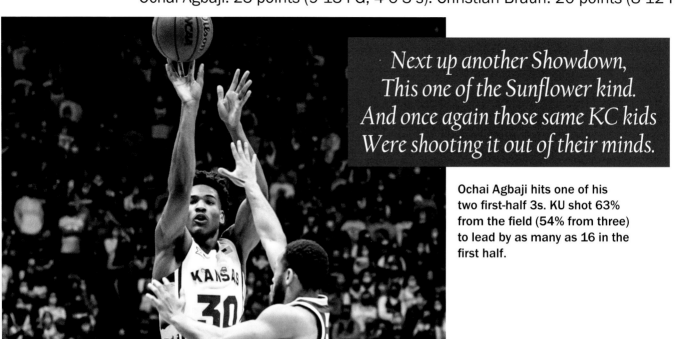

Next up another Showdown,
This one of the Sunflower kind.
And once again those same KC kids
Were shooting it out of their minds.

Ochai Agbaji hits one of his two first-half 3s. KU shot 63% from the field (54% from three) to lead by as many as 16 in the first half.

KU donned special uniforms as part of an "Honoring Black Excellence" initiative.

We like when teams push the pace with us because I don't think any team in the country can play that fast with us. We are a good team in transition, so when good teams want to play like that, we will score 100.
— Christian Braun

43 more from Och and CB,
This time 17 of 25!
Dominance and Efficiency,
As that duo continued to thrive.

Mitch Lightfoot converts a Dajuan Harris Jr. pass into an alley-oop dunk through contact by Kansas State's Ismael Massoud. Lightfoot's ensuing free throw ballooned KU's lead to 25 with 7:40 to play.

KU Athletics Director Travis Goff (right), Associate AD for Inclusive Excellence Paul Pierce II (left) and the fans in Allen Fieldhouse join members of the LaVannes Squires family to recognize a true Kansas Basketball pioneer.

Three Jayhawks, including Christian Braun, hit at least three 3s. KU shot 63% from 3.

at Baylor
80-70 Baylor

Ochai Agbaji: 27 points. Christian Braun: 17 points, 10 rebounds.
David McCormack: 10 points, 13 rebounds.

Christian Braun scores off his offensive rebound. KU's 16 offensive rebounds resulted in 22 second-chance points.

We played a really good team tonight and got beat. It was a missed opportunity because we played so well early.
— Bill Self

Ochai Agbaji drives down the lane through three defenders. KU led by 13 with 5:47 left in the first half but scored just four points the rest of the half and shot 29% from the field in the second.

Then came a Texas-sized setback, Losing two in a row on the road.

at TCU
74-64 TCU

Ochai Agbaji: 13 points, eight rebounds. Jalen Wilson: 13 points, seven rebounds.

Ochai Agbaji tries to rally his team, down seven midway through the second half, with this block of Mike Miles, the second of Ochai's two blocks.

They dominated us on the glass. They're so athletic and long and, of course, we played so unathletic tonight. Really a poor outing. I don't think you could say that anybody really played well. That hasn't happened to us this year at all, I don't think. But they had a lot to do with it.
— Bill Self

Joseph Yesufu pressures Mike Miles on the perimeter. The Horned Frogs played some defense as well, holding KU to 29% shooting in the second half (37% overall). TCU also outrebounded KU, 47-35, and scored 13 second-chance points off of 19 offensive rebounds.

After losses at Baylor and TCU, It was time for the wagons to load.

TCU
72-68 Kansas
Ochai Agbaji: 22 points (8-19 FG). Jalen Wilson: 10 rebounds.

No more margin for error,
Nothing left to spare.
We needed two home wins in just three days
To earn a Big 12 title share.

Christian Braun's 3 with 3:26 left in the second half gave KU a six-point lead and led TCU Coach Jamie Dixon to call timeout.

Mitch Lightfoot produced two steals within two minutes midway through the second half. KU turned 15 TCU turnovers into 25 points.

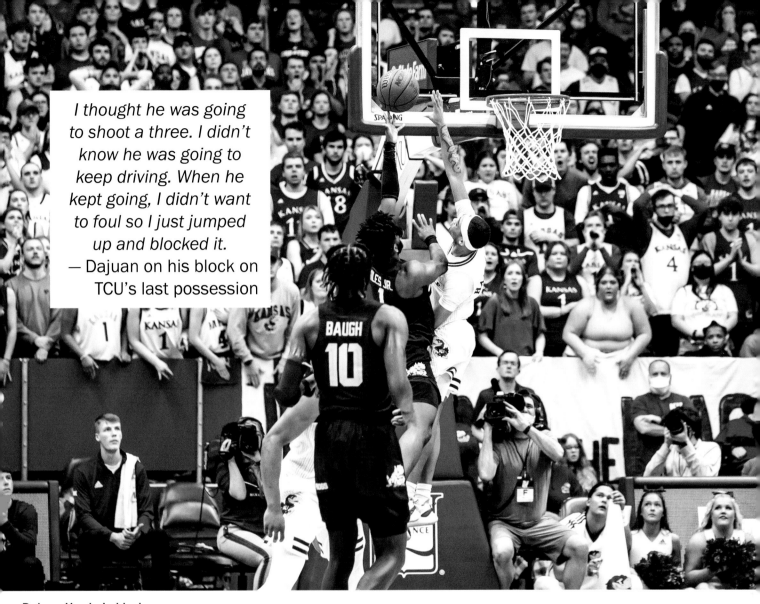

I thought he was going to shoot a three. I didn't know he was going to keep driving. When he kept going, I didn't want to foul so I just jumped up and blocked it.
— Dajuan on his block on TCU's last possession

Dajuan Harris Jr. blocks Mike Miles' layup attempt with five seconds left in the game. KU led by eight with 2:34 to go, but TCU cut it to three with :36 left.

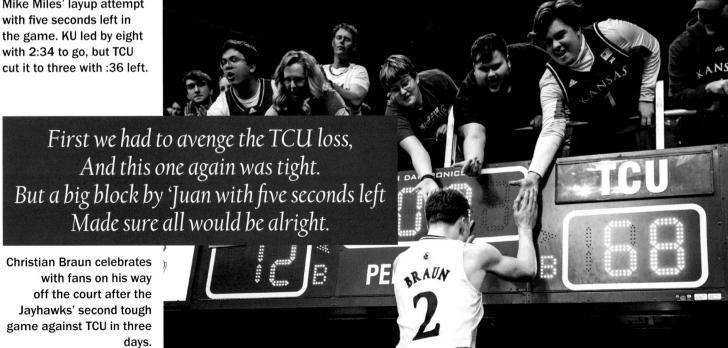

First we had to avenge the TCU loss,
And this one again was tight.
But a big block by 'Juan with five seconds left
Made sure all would be alright.

Christian Braun celebrates with fans on his way off the court after the Jayhawks' second tough game against TCU in three days.

Texas (Senior Day)
70-63 (OT) Kansas

David McCormack: 22 points (6-13 FG, 10-10 FT), 10 rebounds.
Jalen Wilson: 17 points, 13 rebounds. Christian Braun: 13 points, 11 rebounds.

Jalen Coleman-Lands, Remy Martin, Chris Teahan, David McCormack, Ochai Agbaji and Mitch Lightfoot pose for one last group photo on Senior Day.

Bill Self: "Ochai carried KU on his back all year." Ochai Agbaji's eight points moved him into 22nd place on KU's all-time scoring list.

David won us the game. He put us on his back and Jalen had a great night on the glass.
—Bill Self

David McCormack slams home a feed from Ochai Agbaji with 40 seconds left in overtime, giving KU a four-point lead and sealing the victory. McCormack's 10-10 performance at the free-throw line was KU's best since Devonte' Graham went 13-13 against Texas Tech in January 2018.

The league race came down to the Texas game. Could KU win the Big 12 yet again? To clinch a 39th-straight Senior Day, D-Mac, J-Wil and CB all chipped in.

Christian Braun and Jalen Wilson celebrate Braun's 3 with 1:08 to go in the first half that gave KU a brief four-point lead. This seesaw battle saw 16 lead changes and 14 ties.

All three notched double-doubles,
And Kansas kept up its conference winning.

(left) The Jayhawks' victory clinched a share of KU's 20th Big 12 regular-season championship in 26 years. KU has now won on 39 consecutive Senior Days.

Ochai Agbaji delivers his senior speech with the perfect backdrop: KU's 16 Big 12 Championship trophies from the Bill Self era.

A 16th league title in 19 years! But the trophy hunt was just beginning.

Fan favorite Mitch Lightfoot soaks in the love from the Allen Fieldhouse crowd after finishing his thank yous on Senior Day.

Prior to tipoff, Ochai Agbaji receives the 2021-22 Big 12 Player-of-the-Year award from Big 12 Commissioner Bob Bowlsby.

Kansas City native Ochai Agbaji scores over two Mountaineers just minutes down the road from his alma mater, Oak Park High School. Three weeks later, on National Championship Monday, his high school celebrated "Och" Park Day.

Big 12 quarterfinal: West Virginia
87-63 Kansas

Ochai Agbaji: 18 points. Mitch Lightfoot: 10 points (5-6 FG), five blocks.

I think we were all just energized and ready to prove something.
— Ochai Agbaji on KU opening the game on a 24-4 run

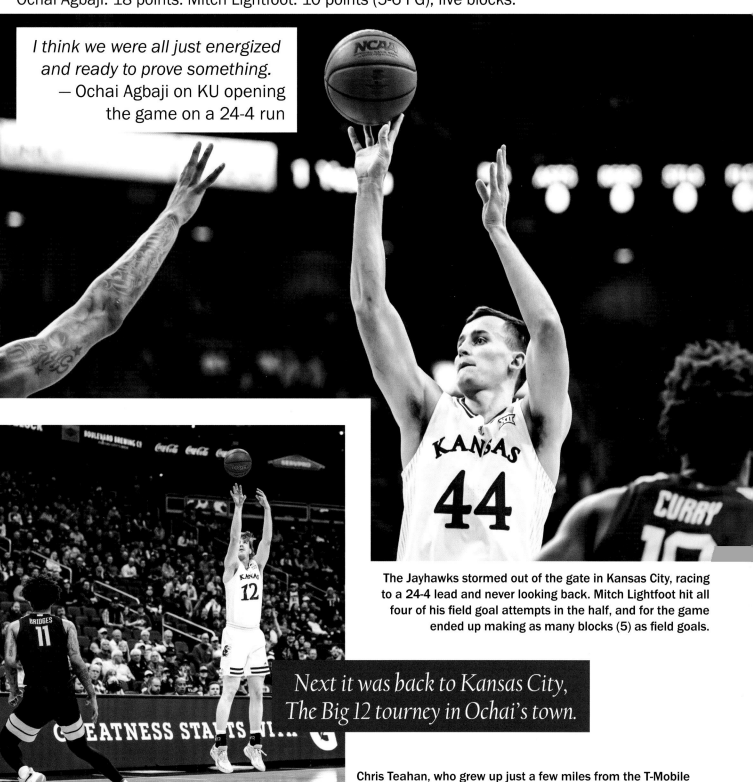

The Jayhawks stormed out of the gate in Kansas City, racing to a 24-4 lead and never looking back. Mitch Lightfoot hit all four of his field goal attempts in the half, and for the game ended up making as many blocks (5) as field goals.

Next it was back to Kansas City, The Big 12 tourney in Ochai's town.

Chris Teahan, who grew up just a few miles from the T-Mobile Center, adds to the blowout by knocking down a 3-pointer.

Big 12 semifinal: TCU
75-62 Kansas

Ochai Agbaji: 22 points (9-17 FG). Mitch Lightfoot: 15 points (6-8 FG).

Mitch Lightfoot stood out early,
But Och's slam brought the whole house down.

Longtime observers of Bill Self's Kansas teams likely saw this one coming. A perfect inbounds pass by Dajuan Harris Jr. from under KU's basket resulted in this prodigious alley-oop dunk by Ochai Agbaji.

It was insane. Ochai might be the highest jumper off of lobs I've ever seen. Like, it's insane. Incredible. Anybody can hit a three, but I don't think anybody else can jump 12-and-a-half feet in the air and dunk that.
— Mitch Lightfoot

Agbaji's awesome dunk stretched KU's second-half lead to 19 and produced a priceless reaction from teammate Mitch Lightfoot that went viral.

Mitch Lightfoot had two of KU's six blocks against TCU, and the Jayhawks pestered the Horned Frogs into 18 turnovers.

A right-hand hammer flushed on the Frogs,
A dunk as vicious as you'll see.
A slam rivaling Selden and Lafrentz,
For best in KU history.

Big 12 Title Game vs. Texas Tech
74-65 Kansas

David McCormack: 18 points, 11 rebounds. Remy Martin: 12 points, four assists, three steals.

I don't think we would've won the game without Remy. I thought he was great.
—Bill Self

*The championship came down
To a rubber match with Tech,
A team known nationally for its defense.
But could they keep Big Dave in check?*

Remy Martin joined four other Jayhawks in double figures, the fourth time this season that five Jayhawks scored 10 or more points.

Dajuan Harris Jr. goes baseline and passes to Ochai Agbaji for a corner 3 – KU's only 3 of the half – to give the Jayhawks a five-point lead early in the second half.

David McCormack floats one in between two defenders. This tense struggle between two teams that know each other well was still a four-point game with under three minutes to go.

*McCormack came up huge in the title game,
Something quickly becoming a theme.*

David McCormack draws a crowd of Red Raiders. His double-double was his 10th of the season, most in the Big 12 Conference.

Bill Self and the Jayhawks celebrate KU's 12th Big 12 Tournament title, and ninth under Self, which solidified the Jayhawks' No. 1 seed in their 50th NCAA Tournament appearance.

I've never cut nets before, and I'm planning to cut a couple more.
— Remy Martin

As the confetti falls, the Jayhawks continue to celebrate. Remy Martin (left) totaled 22 points, seven rebounds, seven assists three steals and zero turnovers in the semis and final (45 combined minutes).

Watching the NCAA Tournament Selection Show, the Big 12 Champs learn they've officially earned the No. 1 seed in the Midwest Region and will start play in Ft. Worth, Texas.

And now armed with yet another 1 seed, It was time to dare to dream.

NCAA First Round vs. Texas Southern
83-56 Kansas

Remy Martin: 15 points (6-8 FG). Christian Braun: 14 points (4-5 3's).

> *Remy's passion adds a lot to our team. We all feed off it. When he plays like that, we're tough to beat.*
> — Christian Braun

Remy Martin converts his own steal into a breakaway first-half dunk, much to the enjoyment of a trailing Ochai Agbaji. Martin helped lead Kansas to its 15th consecutive NCAA first-round victory.

First it was back to Fort Worth, Texas;
The Madness had begun.
The Jayhawks started Remy Marchin',
And man, was Martin fun!

(opposite page) Texas Southern's John Walker can only watch as David McCormack, after stealing the ball from Walker, slams one home to make it 53-24 Kansas four minutes into the second half.

> *Remy was great. He came in and played lights out, terrific.*
> —Bill Self

Remy Martin connected on six of his eight field goal attempts; he also registered four assists and two steals with no turnovers.

Instant "Remergy" off the bench,
While scoring points in bunches.
And as other top seeds started to fall,
Kansas kept dodging punches.

NCAA Second Round vs. Creighton
79-72 Kansas

Remy Martin: 20 points, seven rebounds, four assists. Jalen Wilson: 14 points, 14 rebounds.

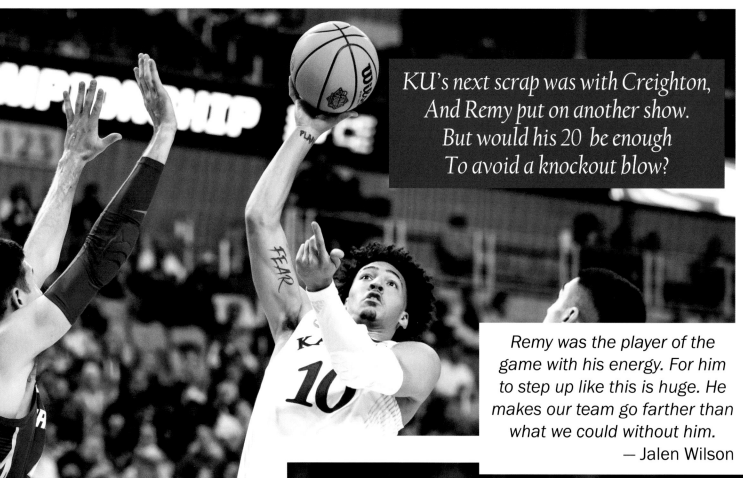

*KU's next scrap was with Creighton,
And Remy put on another show.
But would his 20 be enough
To avoid a knockout blow?*

Remy was the player of the game with his energy. For him to step up like this is huge. He makes our team go farther than what we could without him.
— Jalen Wilson

Jalen Wilson's work at both ends of the floor helped KU reach the 30-victory mark, the 10th time in the Bill Self era (and 16th overall) that Kansas has achieved that feat.

Remy Martin subbed in six minutes into the game, and his floor leadership helped guide KU into the Sweet 16 for the 32nd time in program history. In 50 minutes of action over two games in Ft. Worth he dished out eight assists and committed just one turnover. KU's bench outscored Creighton's, 25-0.

You have to win games when it's kind of ugly, and I don't know that we could've won this game two months ago. I'm proud of our guys.
— Bill Self

One of two second-half blocks by David McCormack, this one led to a Christian Braun fast-break bucket and a six-point KU lead with 16:31 to play.

A one-point game with a minute to play,
The Jays had the Jayhawks on the ropes.
But that's when Ochai stole the ball,
Dashing Creighton's upset hopes.

Consensus All-America First-Team selection Ochai Agbaji races the length of the court after snaring an errant pass. His dunk with :56 to go bumps the KU lead to three, and Creighton would get no closer.

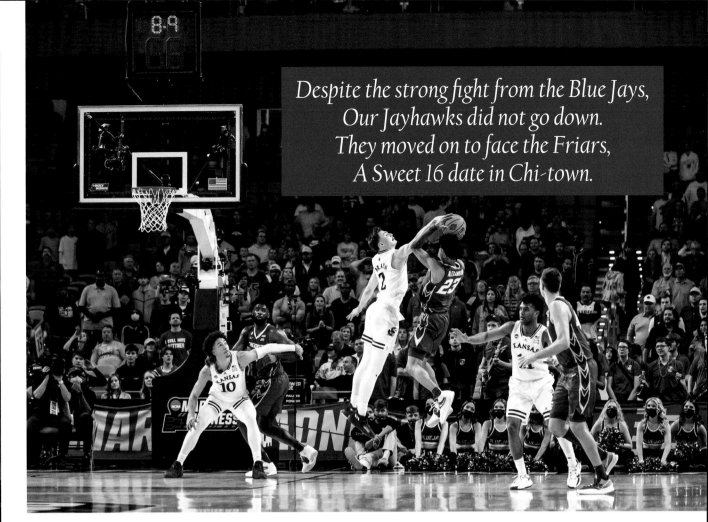

Despite the strong fight from the Blue Jays,
Our Jayhawks did not go down.
They moved on to face the Friars,
A Sweet 16 date in Chi-town.

Setting the stage for another late-game lockdown, Christian Braun pressures Trey Alexander into a turnover in the final seconds to snuff out any hopes of a Creighton comeback. Braun had 13 points, eight rebounds and four assists in a team-leading 38 minutes.

Kansas advanced in the bracket to the 32nd Sweet 16 in program history after a grind-it-out victory over Creighton.

NCAA Sweet 16 vs. Providence
66-61 Kansas

Remy Martin: 23 points, seven rebounds. Jalen Wilson: 16 points, 11 rebounds.

Ochai Agbaji may have had a quiet night offensively (five points), but his defense spoke volumes. He blocked four shots, three of them in the first 5:13 of the game, and had two of KU's three steals. KU held Providence to 17 first-half points, the fewest KU allowed in a half all season and the fewest KU had allowed in a half of an NCAA Tournament game since Ohio U. scored 15 in 1985.

The toughest team will always win. If we play with that mindset and a chip on our shoulder, we can get through any situation, like tonight.
— Jalen Wilson

Some experts then picked Providence,
Because in close games they'd always prevailed.
But when they ran into the Jayhawks,
Their tight-game magic quickly failed.

With Providence clamping down on KU's top two scorers, Remy Martin picked up the slack with 23 points. Buckets were hard to come by in this one: Both teams shot under 40% from the field and under 20% from beyond the arc.

Christian Braun scored just two field goals but came up big with 10 rebounds.

A five-point victory over the Friars
Not only continued KU's climb,
But with that win Kansas became
The winningest program of ALL-TIME!

A happy group of Jayhawks are headed to the NCAA Elite Eight for the 25th time in program history, the eighth under Bill Self. With the victory, Kansas supplanted Kentucky as the winningest basketball program of all time with 2,354 wins.

NCAA Elite 8 vs. Miami
76-50 Kansas

Ochai Agbaji: 18 points (8-12 FG). David McCormack: 15 points (6-7 FG).

Jalen Wilson draws a foul on this first-half jumper. Wilson had an off night shooting, but he grabbed a game-high 11 rebounds and added three assists and a steal. KU trailed by six at the half after being held to 42% shooting, but ran away from the Hurricanes in the second half on the strength of 59% shooting.

With David McCormack providing the block-out, Ochai Agbaji drives for two of his team-high 18 points. KU outscored Miami in the paint, 42-20.

Then came a date with the Hurricanes,
The Elite 8 in the Windy City.
After a slow start for our Jayhawks,
The second half was oh-so-pretty!

David McCormack's signature flex becomes a full-on strut after his and-one off an offensive rebound capped a 10-0 KU run at 14:21 of the second half. KU scored 17 second-chance points; Miami had none.

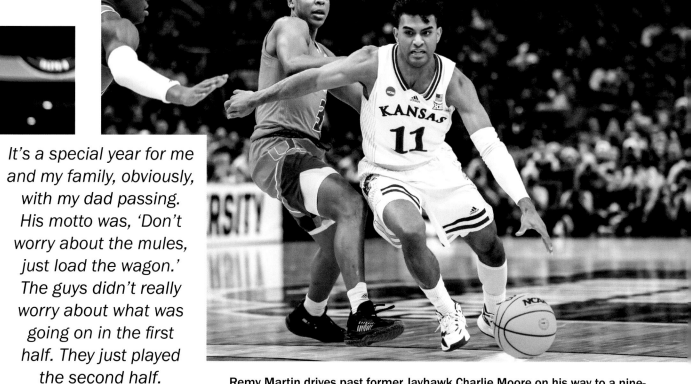

It's a special year for me and my family, obviously, with my dad passing. His motto was, 'Don't worry about the mules, just load the wagon.' The guys didn't really worry about what was going on in the first half. They just played the second half.
— Bill Self

Remy Martin drives past former Jayhawk Charlie Moore on his way to a nine-point, six-rebound, two-assist performance. He committed just one turnover and was named the Most Outstanding Player of the Midwest Regional.

Twenty minutes of dominance,
A 47-15 statement made.
The most convincing half of basketball
Any tourney team had played.

In his core, Remy always knew what he was capable of, but we hadn't seen it yet because of his health. Our guys have more of a swagger now knowing what Remy can do to make us better and that gives us extra confidence.
— Bill Self

Ochai Agbaji's jump shot returned to form against Miami, something that would carry over in a big way in New Orleans.

Super senior Mitch Lightfoot has played in more games at KU than any other Jayhawk. (Miami was his 166th.) Near the end of this one he lets everyone know who's Final Four-bound.

2022 NCAA DIVISION I MEN'S BASKETBALL CHAMPIONSHIP

SWEET 16
MARCH 24-6

ELITE 8'
MARCH 26-27

KANSAS

KANSAS

PROVIDENCE

KANSAS

IOWA STATE

MIAMI (FL)

REGIONAL
CHAMPION

MARCH
MADNESS

SWEET 16
ELITE 8

MIDWEST REGIONAL
CHICAGO

The bracket tells the story: The Midwest Regional champs are headed to the NCAA Final Four, the program's 16th and its fourth with Bill Self at the helm. David McCormack and Christian Braun joined Martin on the Midwest Regional All-Tournament team.

The Jayhawks made it rain in a delirious locker room after storming past the Hurricanes with a 47-15 second-half blitz. The 15 points tied the KU record for second-fewest number of points given up in a half in an NCAA Tournament game. The fewest? Fourteen against Rice in 1940.

Final Four vs. Villanova
81-65 Kansas

David McCormack: 25 points (10-12 FG), nine rebounds. Ochai Agbaji: 21 points (6-8 FG, 6-7 3's).

I'm sure you guys are ready to be done with me, but what do you say we (beat Villanova and) practice once more on Sunday?
—Bill Self, prior to the Villanova game

Next a clash with 'Nova in NOLA,
A Final Four score to settle with Wright.
But unlike 2018 in San Antone',
This was KU's Night.

The Road to the Final Four ends in New Orleans. The last remaining No. 1 seed stepped off its charter flight and was greeted on a carpeted runway by the sweet sounds of a New Orleans jazz band.

In front of 70,000 fans in the Caesars Superdome and millions more on worldwide television, KU's starting lineup huddles up moments before the Final Four begins. Bill Self went with the starting lineup of Ochai Agbaji, Christian Braun, Dajuan Harris Jr., David McCormack and Jalen Wilson for the 23rd time this season.

I was just like, 'If you find me, I'm going to knock it down.' One of those nights. This is what I play for. This is what I work for, just performing in the moment.
— Ochai Agbaji

Ochai Agbaji opens the Final Four scoring with a 3, 19 seconds into the game, letting Villanova know early that he was going to be a problem.

(opposite page) With one of the most ferocious slams of the Final Four, David McCormack posterizes Jermaine Samuels to give KU a 12-point lead with 10:34 to go. The Jayhawks shot 54% from the field against a team that this season allowed its opponents just 41%.

Ochai came out scorching hot.
Six straight threes, hotter than the sun!
And McCormack again was oh-so-clutch:
25 and 9, when all was said and done.

Ochai Agbaji hit his first six 3s, including four in the first eight minutes, a one-man barrage reminiscent of Villanova's shooting performance against KU to open the 2018 Final Four.

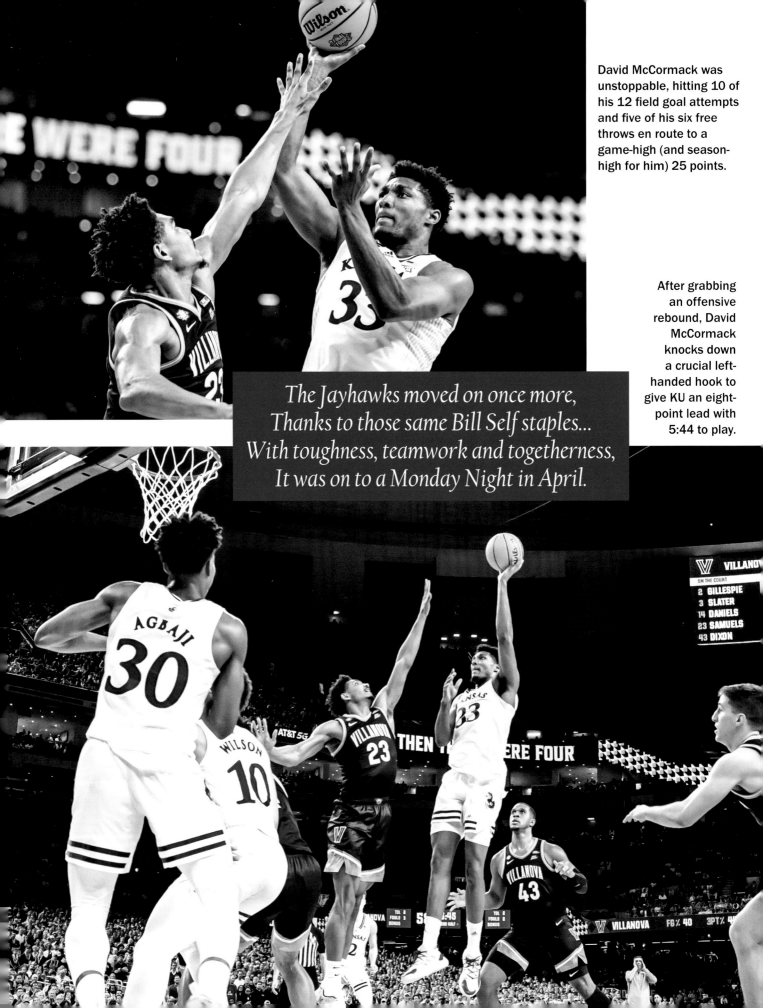

David McCormack was unstoppable, hitting 10 of his 12 field goal attempts and five of his six free throws en route to a game-high (and season-high for him) 25 points.

After grabbing an offensive rebound, David McCormack knocks down a crucial left-handed hook to give KU an eight-point lead with 5:44 to play.

The Jayhawks moved on once more,
Thanks to those same Bill Self staples...
With toughness, teamwork and togetherness,
It was on to a Monday Night in April.

Christian Braun's 3 with four minutes to go gave KU a 12-point lead, and the Wildcats would get no closer.

We're grateful for the opportunity but we've got unfinished business. We've got one more to go and that's the first thing everyone said. We're not satisfied.
—Christian Braun

Ochai Agbaji is fouled on this layup attempt; he hit one of two free throws to extend KU's lead to 72-59 with 3:31 to go.

Mitch Lightfoot reminds his teammates: "We've still got one more to go." Monday night's championship game will be his 17th career NCAA Tournament game, more than any player in Kansas basketball history.

Only one opponent left to go,
The dream so close to being real.
But to hang that elusive sixth banner,
We had to chill those hot Tarheels.

The final practice Coach Self hoped for. The Jayhawks prepare on Sunday for North Carolina.

National Championship vs. North Carolina
72-69 Kansas

David McCormack: 15 points, 10 rebounds. Jalen Wilson: 15 points.
Remy Martin: 14 points (4-6 3's). Christian Braun: 12 points, 12 rebounds.

Amidst sparkling fireworks and billowing smoke, Ochai Agbaji leads the Jayhawks onto the Caesars Superdome floor.

Opening tip: David McCormack outjumps his former AAU teammate, North Carolina's Armando Bacot.

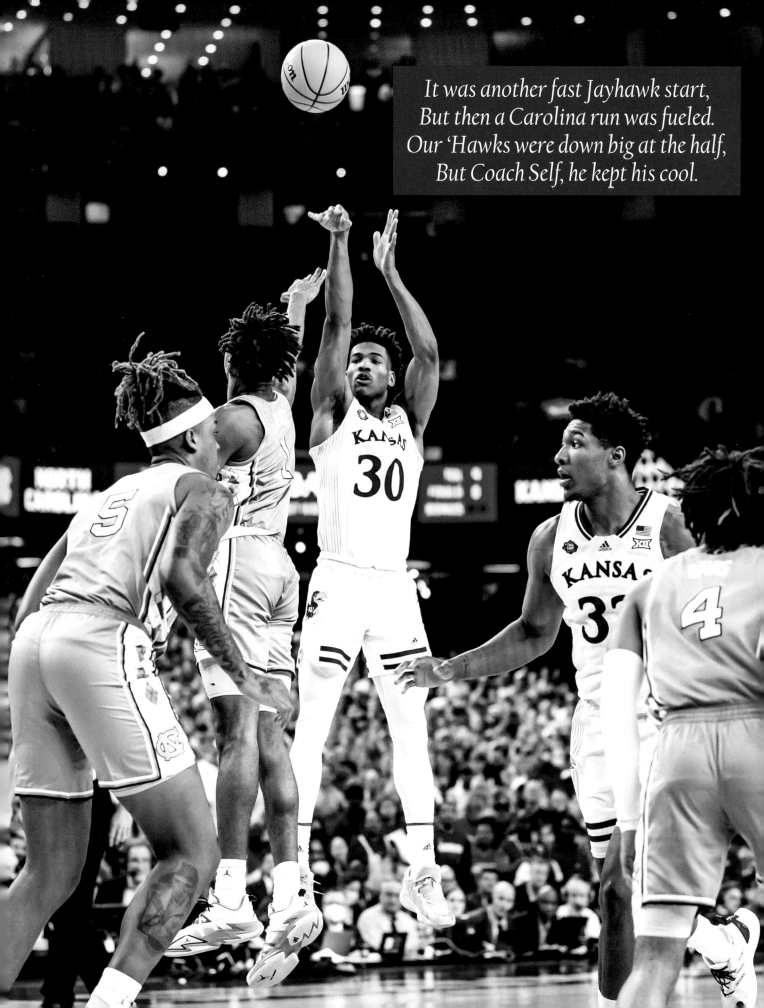

It was another fast Jayhawk start,
But then a Carolina run was fueled.
Our 'Hawks were down big at the half,
But Coach Self, he kept his cool.

UNC's Armando Bacot had 12 points and 10 rebounds by halftime, securing his 31st double-double of the season, tying David Robinson's NCAA single-season record set more than 30 years ago. David McCormack and the Jayhawks held him without a field goal in the second half.

(opposite page) Ochai Agbaji picks up right where he left off against Villanova. He opened the championship game with a three-pointer 13 seconds into the game.

Finishes were tough to come by for KU in the first half. Jalen Wilson misfires from close-in, one of 15 Jayhawk misses from inside the paint in the first 20 minutes. KU went to the locker room shooting just 30 percent.

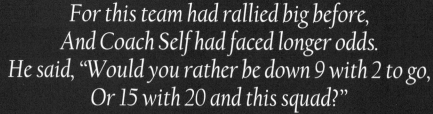

For this team had rallied big before,
And Coach Self had faced longer odds.
He said, "Would you rather be down 9 with 2 to go,
Or 15 with 20 and this squad?"

Amid a UNC run, Ochai Agbaji receives encouragement from Bill Self.

I asked them that at halftime, because that's obviously what happened in 2008. They all said, 'Let's take 15,' and we played off of that.
— Bill Self

Wilson, Agbaji, Braun and the rest of the Jayhawks were determined to turn things around in the second half, spurred on by motivational words from Coach Bill Self.

THE ROAD ENDS HERE

Christian Braun hit two huge layups in less than 40 seconds midway through the second half, both times getting the Jayhawks to within one.

That sparked a Kansas comeback,
Unlike college hoops had ever seen.
The largest one in title game history,
We rallied back from down FIFTEEN!

Jalen Wilson contributed 11 points, three rebounds and two assists to KU's remarkable second-half comeback.

Another total team effort;
CB racked up a quick ten.
Jalen's shots were hitting too.
The 'Hawks were cookin' again!

When we saw our own blood, we didn't panic. We came out the second half coming in hot.
— Bill Self

Christian Braun goes coast-to-coast early in the second half as the Jayhawks start the long road back from a 15-point halftime deficit.

Braun reacts with the crowd after his layup at 12:44 of the second half brought the Jayhawks to within one, 46-45. Down 15 at the half, KU took just 7:16 to trim the deficit to one.

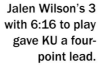

Jalen Wilson's 3 with 6:16 to play gave KU a four-point lead.

Then another classic Remy run;
Corner Pocket three balls were fallin'.
Next a crossover, step-back three.
That Martin kid was ballin'.

After banking in a three and going one-for-five in the first half, Remy Martin shot the lights out in the second, hitting all four of his shots (three-for-three from beyond the arc).

(opposite page) At 10:21 of the second half, Remy Martin hits a corner 3 to give KU a 53-50 lead. The Jayhawks hadn't led since 9:43 of the first half (18-16).

With just under a minute to go, Remy Martin denies Caleb Love's layup attempt to preserve KU's one-point lead.

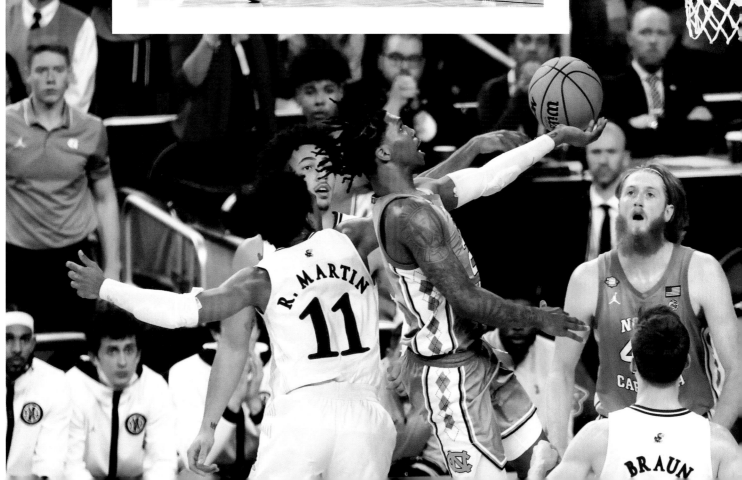

> *Och was huge and so was 'Juan.*
> *But when they needed this game saved,*
> *The 'Hawks fed it to McCormack,*
> *And most outstanding was Big Dave.*

Ochai Agbaji draws attention from a crowd of Tar Heels as he tries to extend KU's four-point lead with under six minutes to play.

Dajuan Harris Jr. whips a pass inside during KU's furious rally. He had two of KU's eight second-half assists.

David McCormack follows his own miss – the last of his 10 rebounds – and gives KU the lead for good with 1:21 left.

I don't really care because we won the national championship, but if I really had to choose a most outstanding player throughout the entire Final Four, it would be David.
—Ochai Agbaji

After Martin's block, David McCormack hits another huge bucket in the lane to stretch KU's lead to three with :22 to play. The media had submitted its Most Outstanding Player ballots before David hit his two crucial buckets, but his coaches and teammates believed he and Ochai could have been co-MOPs.

Together this special Jayhawk group
Made KU Hoops history,
Delivering another Banner Year,
Thanks to elite team chemistry.

Christian Braun and KJ Adams Jr. stretch to defend Caleb Love's last-ditch effort to tie the game.

They really care for each other. It's the closest-knit group. We've had some great teams, but I don't think we've had a team closer than this team.
— Bill Self

Coach Bill Self exults at the final buzzer as his Jayhawks secure their place in Kansas history.

KU's championship celebration commences as a shower of crimson and blue confetti begins to fall.

This is a special group of guys. We're going down in history. All I've got to say is, 'Rock Chalk, baby!'
— Ochai Agbaji

Two huge pieces of the Jayhawks' 2021-22 puzzle, Christian Braun and Ochai Agbaji, embrace on the court as confetti rains down in the background after KU's record-setting second-half comeback.

Jalen Wilson and Christian Braun make confetti angels below the podium during the postgame celebration.

A happy group of Jayhawks complete their perfect bracket with Kansas on top.

Coach Bill Self and his Jayhawks finally get their hands on what they worked toward all year as they hoist the 2022 NCAA Men's Basketball Championship trophy.

We just locked in as a family, as a team, and that's what we do. We overcome the odds. We overcome adversity. We're just built for this.
— David McCormack

Memories we'll cherish for a lifetime,
Achievements that have us all braggin'.
And all because they didn't worry about the mules;
These Jayhawks Just Loaded the Wagon.

2022 NATIONAL CHAMPIONS

Kansas fans will forever cherish this Banner Year, but what did playing a role in the title run mean to each Jayhawk? How about the significance of adding to the illustrious history of Kansas Basketball? Finally, besides the National Championship game, what was everyone's favorite moment of the season? Each National Champion Jayhawk shares their answers in the pages ahead.

0 *Bobby Pettiford*

6-1 190 FR
Guard
Durham, NC
Season High: 5 points (vs. Michigan State in NYC)

It meant everything to me to be a part of the National Championship team. Growing up that's something you would only dream of, and honestly, it still doesn't feel real to me yet. Being a part of something like that can set you up for a lifetime and put you in positions you didn't know you could be in.

My favorite moment of the season besides the Natty was the Big 12 Championship game. That win over Texas Tech really brought our team together. It gave us the confidence and the boost we needed. It showed how tough we were and that we could trust our brothers inside those lines.

1 Joseph Yesufu

6-0 180 Soph
Guard
Bolingbrook, IL
Season High: 9 points (vs. Iona in Orlando & vs. Kansas State)

Being a part of this National Championship run meant a lot not only to me but also to my loved ones. Being a part of a great group of guys who pushed you every day to be the best you could be was really special. Getting to help add to the KU tradition is an honor. There have been many legends come through here and it's important to keep that tradition going.

My favorite moment other than the title game was beating Mizzou and the awesome atmosphere we had in the Phog that day.

#1

2 Christian Braun

6-7 218 JR
Guard
Burlington, KS
Season High: 31 (at St. John's)

Being from Kansas, I think the title means a little bit more to me. I had one goal when I decided to go to Kansas and that was to win a National Championship.

It means a lot to add to the tradition at Kansas because we worked hard for it and did it the right way. I got to do it with people I love and for people that mean a lot to me. I had a lot of fun accomplishing what we achieved all year.

My favorite part of the season was the doubt that some people had in us before the season and at other times throughout the year. We had a lot of people telling us for our whole careers what we couldn't do, and that just made it even more special when we won it all. Everyone on the team had something to prove, and it added to our personality as a team. I just enjoyed being from Kansas and winning at Kansas.

3 Dajuan Harris Jr.

6-1 170 RS-Soph
Guard
Columbia, MO
Season High: 14 points (vs. Nevada & at Iowa State)

It meant the world to me winning a championship at KU. It's always been my dream to win a title ever since I first watched the tourney as a child – it's the biggest tournament ever. I used to create myself on video games and help KU win championships, so to know I've now won it all in real life means the world to me.

It means a lot to add to this tradition because this tradition is a family. Every year since I've been here, my teammates and coaches have brought me in and always kept it real.

My favorite memory other than the title game was my game-winning layup against Iowa State, but if I had to pick a second favorite memory it would definitely be beating Mizzou.

5 Kyle Cuffe Jr.

6-2 180 FR
Guard
Harlem, NY
Season High: (DNP)

The title means the world to me and to be a part of it is amazing. Even though I redshirted this past season, I still got to feel what it was like to be a part of a championship program. Helping add to the KU tradition is special because at KU we win, and winners are always going to prosper.

My favorite memory other than the title game was the big home win over Missouri and the atmosphere in the Fieldhouse that day.

10 Jalen Wilson

6-8 215 RS-Soph
Forward
Denton, TX
Season High: 23 points (vs. West Virginia)

Being a part of the title means everything to me. All the dedication and sacrifices that we all made, made it come together and helped us realize that one goal that we had all year. That's something very special that I will never forget.

The KU tradition is very important, and we were able to appreciate how much winning impacts our school. Being able to represent our school in the best manner possible and show Jayhawk fans what our school is about was a very important thing for us.

Besides the win over UNC, I would say my favorite moments of the season were celebrating wins in the locker room with my teammates.

11 Remy Martin

6-0 180 SR
Guard
Chatsworth, CA
Season High: 23 points (vs. Providence at Sweet 16)

Winning a title is the reason we play the game. We work extremely hard to fulfill a goal that not many can say they accomplished. Getting to add to the KU tradition is surreal. All the great players and great teams that have come through and left their mark – to be a part of that brotherhood is a real honor.

My favorite memory is when I was actually healthy enough to play and thinking to myself, 'The world has no idea what I'm about to do this month of March!' And y'all know the rest.

#22

12 *Chris Teahan*

6-4 195 Super-SR
Guard
Leawood, KS
Season High: 3 points (vs. Tarleton St., vs. Missouri & vs. West Virginia)

Being a part of the title is a dream I've had since I was a kid. It still doesn't feel real and has taught me many valuable lessons that changed my life. Kansas is the best college program in the world. As a Kansas kid, being able to be on a team that will forever be remembered was one of the most important goals when I first showed up on campus.

My favorite memory outside of the Natty is the bus ride home from the K-State game. It's when we all knew we could be special. It meant a lot to me and I know it meant a lot to all the upperclassmen before who have had tough draws in their careers.

13 Charlie McCarthy

6-2 195 FR
Guard
Rancho Mirage, CA
Season High: DNP

Winning the title with this group of guys was the best moment of my life. It's an experience I will think about every day for the rest of my life. Even months later, it still feels surreal.

Growing up a diehard KU Basketball fan, getting to add to the tradition with a National Championship means the world to me. The tradition and history of Kansas Basketball is unrivaled and I'm so thankful that I'm now a part of it. There's no place like Kansas.

My favorite moment this season, other than the championship game, was the double-overtime win over Texas Tech in Allen Fieldhouse. That game really showed how tough and gritty our team is.

15 Dillon Wilhite

6-9 240 FR
Forward
San Diego, CA
Season High: DNP

A championship is the pinnacle of success for every basketball player. To spend every year since I was 5 years old playing basketball and dreaming of March Madness makes the win even more sweet. No matter how big or small your part was, we couldn't have made it there without each other. Our season solidified for me that a team is only as good as the sum of its parts, and in 2022 it all added up for KU Basketball! I feel great knowing that I will always be part of Jayhawk basketball history. To be in the brotherhood of outstanding players who will come back to campus in future years and be able to look back on our championship season is a huge honor.

Can I have more than one favorite memory? Because the whole season was packed full of them – Late Night, battling for wins every week, police escorts for the team bus, Kansas-wrapped buses in NOLA, cheering fans lining the streets, the craziness of Final Four down on the floor, confetti falling and One Shining Moment playing, climbing the ladder to cut down the net, and our parade down Mass. Street – it was a season I'll never forget!

20 Michael Jankovich

6-5 190 JR
Guard
Dallas, TX
Season High: 3 points (vs. Stony Brook & vs. UTEP in KC)

Being a part of a National Championship team is so special because there is so much that goes into it and it's something that very few people get to experience. The run we had will be remembered for many years to come and that is something that can't be understated.

As a kid who spent a few years living in Lawrence, KU Basketball was everything to me. All I can remember was going to games, spending time in the Fieldhouse and wanting to be a part of it someday. Having the opportunity to become part of the tradition here is a dream come true.

My favorite memory of the season was just the relationships that I built with my teammates over the course of the year. This group was probably the closest team I've ever been a part of, and those friendships are something that will last a lifetime.

21 Zach Clemence

6-10 225 FR
Forward
San Antonio, TX
Season High: 11 points (vs. Stony Brook)

I will now forever be a part of the tradition, and this title run was one of the greatest feelings and accomplishments I've ever been a part of.

I have so many great memories from the season, but my favorite memory is the KU vs. Oklahoma game. I had been out for weeks because of an injury, but Coach called me off the bench to play and I was ready. I have to give it my all every time I touch that floor. I'm here to win and when given the opportunity, I'm taking it. My team needed me and I guarded Groves to stop him. Plus, my 3-pointer was icing on the cake! I will take that kind of game anytime.

Clemence
#21

24 *KJ Adams Jr.*

6-7 220 FR
Forward
Austin, TX
Season High: 6 points (vs. Iona in Orlando & vs. Texas Tech)

Winning the National Championship is something you dream of as a kid but dreams like that rarely come true. So to be on the floor as the buzzer sounded saying that we were National Champs was the fulfillment of what I've dreamed of for a very long time. I chose Kansas because of its great history in the game of basketball, so being a part of that history now is pretty exciting.

My favorite memory is starting on the floor in double-overtime versus Texas Tech and making big plays to help us win that game in Allen Fieldhouse. Nothing, though, beats being on the floor in the final seconds of the national title game and helping us get that last stop to secure the championship.

30 Ochai Agbaji

6-5 214 SR
Guard
Kansas City, MO
Season High: 37 points (vs. Texas Tech)

Winning a National Championship is something every athlete dreams of accomplishing. To finally reach this dream, man, it's so surreal. And even better, I got to experience it with my guys! It means everything to get to add to the KU tradition. Knowing that I played a small part in making history is something I'll be forever proud of!

My favorite memory is probably our comeback win at K-State and all that it meant to Coach and our entire team. It was one of the pivotal turning points of the season that led us to an eventual National Championship. For us to fight all the way back and for me to hit the game-winning shot against our rivals will be one of my lasting memories. It won't just be remembered for the comeback, though. That win was for Coach Self and his father.

31 Cam Martin

6-9 230 Super-SR
Forward
Yukon, OK
Season High: DNP

Being a part of a National Championship team means the world to me. At the beginning of each season that is every team's goal, and to be able to come back to Allen Fieldhouse and see the banner in the rafters forever is a dream come true. KU is such a tradition-rich program, so any time you're able to add to the history it means a lot.

My favorite memory of the season would be the win at Kansas State when we were down big at halftime. Seeing our team fight through that adversity and come back and win the game, not only for us but for Coach Self and his family, is something I'll never forget.

33 David McCormack

6-10 250 SR
Norfolk, VA
Forward
Season High: 25 points (vs. Villanova at Final Four)

Achieving a National Championship is a feeling like no other. It is the absolute farthest one can go in a basketball season, and I was honored to do it with my brothers at KU. It's such blessing to take part in it.

As a lot of people already know, Kansas is the embodiment of basketball history. To now say that I am not only a part of that history, but also added to it, makes me feel I have left the most positive imprint on the program.

Of course there will be a lot of memories that I will cherish, but besides the UNC game, I think the Villanova Final Four game, especially when I posterized a guy on the biggest stage in college basketball, has to be another top-tier memory.

44 Mitch Lightfoot

6-8 225 SR
Forward
Gilbert, AZ
Season High: 15 points (vs. TCU at Big 12 Tournament)

Being a part of the title season is something that I will never forget. The hard work of our players, coaches and staff is something that I will admire and always remember about this team! Coach Self always talks about leaving this place a better place than when you found it, and I took great pride in making sure that happened during my tenure at Kansas. I will always be proud to be a Jayhawk!

My favorite memory other than the championship was the perseverance our team showed being down 16 at the half in hostile territory at K-State. That one was for Coach and I think everyone on our team agrees with that.

55 Jalen Coleman-Lands

6-4 190 Super-SR
Guard
Indianapolis, IN
Season High: 20 points (vs. George Mason)

Winning the title and being a part of it has and will forever be a symbolic reminder of the power of process. But by far the most important takeaway has been the bond I have made with my Jayhawk family. Helping add to the KU tradition will forever create a tie that can never be erased.

My favorite moment was probably my almost-buzzer beater against Texas on Senior Night. Allen was so electric that night and we had so much to play for, given they had beaten us earlier. We were competing for a regular-season championship, and it was Senior Night.

Bill Self

Head Coach

I honestly think I had as much fun coaching this group as any team I've ever coached. They just gave so much of themselves for each other. They had a special closeness about them that made them so much fun to be around. I'm so proud of how hard they worked, how resilient they were, and how they played like men. We weren't always a perfect team, but we played perfectly when it mattered most. Our guys arrived here as caretakers of KU's great basketball history and left this program better than they found it. They'll now be celebrated as one of the most beloved teams in our program's history.

The K-State game was my favorite win other than the title game. It was basically 30 hours after dad had passed and of all the teams out there that he probably wished we'd beat, K-State was always right at the top of that list. I knew that would have meant a lot to him, especially the way we won it – coming from behind – and also competing against a team that, in his mind, was not his favorite.

Kurtis Townsend
Assistant Coach

It was special to be a small part of this title run. Jayhawk Nation was so proud to not only get a National Championship but also to become the all-time winningest program. It was all so surreal. For me to have my wife, my kids, my grandkids and nieces in New Orleans was great. Success is nothing if you don't have loved ones to share it with.

My favorite game of the year was at K-State. Coach's dad had passed away the day before. We played an awful first half but came back and won in the second half after being down big. For 19 years Coach Self has lifted us up daily and to see the team lift him up that day was inspiring. All I could think about was, 'Don't worry about the mules, just load the wagon.'

Norm Roberts
Assistant Coach

Getting to play a role in bringing a sixth National Championship here is obviously a blessing. It's been great for me. I've been with Coach a number of years and we've come close many times – I've been with him for seven Elite 8's – so to be able to get to a Final Four in 2018 and then now win it all in 2022 is pretty awesome.

Everybody talks about the game, but the best moment for me was the night before the game when we met with the team to go over the scouting report for the last time. We had a hype video, which we called *Inches*. We showed that and then right after that we also showed a video that had at least 12-15 former players who spoke about how much it meant to them for our guys to be in this situation and how proud they were of them. I thought that was by far the coolest thing I'd ever experienced and it was really, really emotional, so I got a lot from that.

The game, the celebration with the confetti coming down and all, that was great, but that Sunday night before was unbelievable. It really was.

Jeremy Case

Assistant Coach

Being a part of this championship team means so much to me. It's hard to put it into words. This team, and the way they prevailed when adversity hit, is something I'll never forget. I'll cherish these moments for the rest of my life.

Outside of the championship game, my favorite game moment was against Texas Tech at home— when Ochai hit the 3-pointer to go to a second overtime. That game was such a battle and the crowd was amazing. It was a small sign of what was to come when adversity hit our guys.

Fred Quartlebaum

Director of Basketball Operations

All year the team remained connected, committed and competitive despite the ups and downs that align with the grind of the season. We never overlooked the core of our success, our culture and our belief in one another.

On the last day of boot camp, our Team IMPACT teammate, JP Bemberger, showed up at 6 a.m., and did a down and back using his walker. Observing his KU teammates rally, cheer, clap and will him on from end line to end line is a memory I'll cherish forever.

Brennan Bechard
Director of Student-Athlete Development

It means so much to me to be a part of another Championship team here at KU, especially since I grew up a diehard Jayhawk fan. There are so many highs and lows when a season doesn't end how you want it to. I've seen how truly hard it is to win it all. Winning a championship as a player and now as a member of the coaching staff is pretty surreal. We had so much fun during the tournament, and we couldn't have asked for a better group of guys to go on this championship journey with.

One of my favorite memories outside of the NCAA tournament would have to be the game in Manhattan — and more specifically the locker room afterwards. Everyone knows what Coach Self was going through at the time, and the emotion in there was really special. The high of

coming all the way back, silencing all their fans, and seeing what it meant to Coach Self after the game was really awesome. I think that was a huge moment to bring our team closer together.

Brady Morningstar (left) and Brennan Bechard.

Brady Morningstar
Video Coordinator

I must thank Coach Self first for allowing me to come back and be on staff. What an amazing opportunity this is to learn from the best once again. To be a part of another National Championship team means everything to me. It was so cool to be a part of such a special group. To watch them perform the way they did all season speaks to the team chemistry and the hours of hard work these guys put in daily. Coach challenged the guys all year and they stepped up every time, especially in the second half against Carolina!

The win at Kansas State hands down was my favorite win of the year, and I think we all know why. Just load the wagon, baby! What a win, and what a locker room afterwards!

Bill Cowgill

Associate Director, Sports Medicine

Being part of this championship team was so special knowing what most of this group had gone through from the beginning of the pandemic through that Monday night. Their drive and dedication to reach their ultimate goal amazed me. David McCormack, for example, sometimes logged 4-5 hours a day in the athletic training room to get ready to practice and play. Helping these players and coaches to reach the pinnacle of college basketball is something that I never take for granted.

I have two memories. The first is coming back to beat K-State. We all felt how special that was for Coach Self with the week he had just been through. It was a true family moment in that locker room after the game. The other was sharing this amazing ride with our long-time team physician and my great friend, Larry Magee, who was supposed to retire last December. Coach Self and I talked him into staying through the season, and I'm so glad this team sent him out on top.

Dr. Ramsey Nijem

Director of Sports Performance

Being a part of this championship team was truly special. The way we came back to win was really symbolic of our season. Winning the ultimate prize capped off a year of overcoming so many challenges, both individual and team. I couldn't be happier for our players, coaches, university, and fans. To be a member of this is something I will cherish forever. Our guys were focused, and it was clear all season that we were aligned with one mission. To watch these young men buy in, allow us to coach them, and sacrifice their individual goals for the team is the epitome of sport. I thank them for allowing me to share this journey with them.

So many memories come to mind but a few worth mentioning are the comeback at Kansas State and what that meant for Coach Self, the double-overtime win at home versus Texas Tech, the final conference game overtime win versus Texas to secure the Big 12 title, and obviously, every game in March was incredible.

Travis Goff
Director of Athletics

This season was surreal in so many ways. This team had been through so much together, and Bill and his staff squeezed everything they could from a group of tremendous young men. They were selfless, dedicated to each other, resilient and the very best representatives the University of Kansas could ever ask for. Our dedicated fans – the best in sport – lifted this group up during a tough stretch and, coming through the pandemic, it was amazing to have the Jayhawk nation back together again in Allen Fieldhouse, in KC for the Big 12 Championship, and then to Fort Worth, Chicago and New Orleans. For me, Nancy and our three children, it was even more special (you might even say "lagniappe") as we had spent our previous 17 years in Chicago and New Orleans. More than anything, what this team achieved this year reminded me of something that I will never take for granted – Kansas Basketball is one of the greatest brands and traditions in the history of sport, and it is truly a privilege to be a very small part of this extraordinary program.

There were so many special moments this season. For me, the win on the road in Manhattan in January was like no other. The rivalry is real – you know just how badly their fans want to beat us in basketball – and to then stage an epic comeback down 17 in a hostile environment... Wow. But that all pales in comparison to knowing what Bill had gone through in the days leading up to the game with the loss of his father and how much that win meant to him. I sat at the scorer's table next to the team bench and Bill had a remarkable calmness and sense of confidence even when we dug such a deep hole. He never flinched. And because of that, our guys never lost faith that they could come back and win the game. It was very clear that our guys were more motivated than ever to win that game for Coach Self. It was a special night that I will never forget.

Chancellor Douglas Girod

Upon returning from New Orleans, there was a palpable pride across the state, region and country from Jayhawks of course, but many others as well. It was the talk of the Kansas Statehouse and the Governor's mansion, and in Washington D.C. with our federal delegation. And the parade on Massachusetts Street the weekend after the championship game was one of the truly special moments in KU history. This level of excitement and connectivity significantly enhances the university's brand, visibility and reputation at all levels.

My favorite memory besides the championship game? Certainly it has to be the opportunity to connect with Jayhawks from around the world at our pregame events. In particular, our pep rallies at the House of Blues in NOLA were the thing of legends. Truly an epic experience not to be forgotten!

Afterword
by David McCormack

It was a long and winding road that led to becoming a National Champion. A journey filled with plenty of adversity, triumphs, setbacks, teamwork and togetherness. The path to achieving my hoop dreams wasn't always like I forecasted it, but considering where it took me – and that we finished on top of the college basketball world – I wouldn't change a thing.

At the end of my senior year in high school, my fellow Jayhawk recruits and I received numerous honors, including being named McDonald's All-Americans. So, expectations for our KU team going into my freshman year were extremely high.

At the same time, I was a little nervous having to follow Kansas' 2018 Final Four run. Another expectation to live up to was "The Streak." We did not want to be the team that broke Coach Self's 14-year run of Big 12 regular-season titles. Many preseason polls had us No. 1, so I just knew we would have a great shot at a National Championship.

Sadly, though, throughout the year we faced considerable adversity in the form of injuries. Udoka Azubuike suffered a few injuries, pushing me to step into a more significant role. I definitely loved having the opportunity to play more, but I didn't think it was what we needed going into the postseason.

With the combination of adversity and the pressure of high expectations, my freshman year did not go as I had wanted; KU's 14-year Big 12 Championship streak ended, and Auburn beat us in the second round of March Madness.

A Disney Dunk: Although we didn't win the tourney, it was fun to play in Orlando, where the NBA Bubble took place in 2020.

I was psyched to be opening another home schedule in Allen Fieldhouse. My five blocks were just icing on the cake.

As I entered my sophomore year, we as a team knew we had a lot of things to correct. Azubuike came back from his injury, we adjusted our playing style and we felt very confident going into the year.

We opened the 2019-20 season against Duke at Madison Square Garden, and it was not a pretty game. We committed a whopping 28 turnovers but still only lost by two. There was hope that if we played smart and defended, we could beat anyone. A couple of weeks later we played in the Maui Invitational. Having the opportunity to travel to Maui was amazing in itself, and we also got to play in front of an awesome, electric crowd. We made it to the championship game. It reminded me of a high school tournament game – small gym, loud crowd, and massive energy everywhere. We beat Dayton in a hard-fought overtime game and got to take home the trophy – a surfboard! (Unfortunately, Dayton got revenge against us in an early-season tournament my senior year!)

Fast forward to right before winter break, we played at Villanova. Every player knows it's always best to go home with a win before winter break. Yet again, the game came down to the wire and we lost by a single point. After we came back from break, it was time to really lock in because we were headed to conference play. We all wanted revenge for losing the streak the previous year. Collectively, we were really hitting our stride. Everyone was invested in their roles, and it was working.

Our biggest game of the season came in late February. No. 3 Kansas at No. 1 Baylor – at Baylor in front of ESPN's College GameDay. Everyone thought that whoever won this game would win

the conference. Two things happened that day: First, the Kansas Jayhawks were absolutely in the zone and played phenomenally. Azubuike finished with 23 points and 19 rebounds, while Marcus Garett absolutely shut down anybody in front of him. Second, I think I set a world record for the fastest time to foul out in a game – five fouls in four minutes. We won by three, and the momentum carried through the rest of the regular season, allowing us to reclaim the Big 12 Championship.

Next on the agenda was the Big 12 Tournament, and I will never forget how quickly things unraveled. Everyone was suiting up for our first game, ankles taped, warm-ups on, and about to head to the arena. As we prepared to leave the hotel the news broke that some NBA players had caught Covid-19 and the league had decided to cancel its games. Suddenly we received a text telling us to wait before heading to

I had a few dunks against West Virginia at home, but I was most proud of my 10 offensive rebounds.

the bus. Shortly thereafter came the update: The game, and the rest of the Big 12 Tournament, were canceled. We all were in complete shock.

In a little less than an hour everyone was packed up and the team headed back to Lawrence. With frequent updates, Coach Self let us know that it didn't look good for the NCAA Tournament. As a team we went from the undisputed No. 1 team in America to a team that was denied the opportunity to pursue the National Championship that we and a lot of people in the know thought we could win. Within 48 hours, everyone was back home in quarantine. The lesson for me: Never take anything for granted, because it can all be taken away from you before you have time to truly appreciate what you have.

Like everyone else, I felt the frustration of not being able to move around freely because of the restrictions imposed to combat the global pandemic. After six months of at-home workouts, away from my coaches and teammates, it was finally time to report back to Kansas to begin another season. This season I would step into a new role, one in which I would be the face of the Kansas frontcourt. My teammates and I put forth a lot of effort, dedication and hard work toward having a dominant season. As many may know, the start of the season did not go as planned – Gonzaga whipped us in Florida. Then when we returned to Lawrence, we all had to make a major adjustment: Covid-19-related restrictions greatly reduced the number of fans allowed into Allen Fieldhouse. This felt very strange to me and the other veterans on the team, having already played two years in the loudest indoor arena in the country.

As the season progressed with its multiple peaks and valleys, I began to feel an abnormal discomfort in my foot. Being proactive, I did a normal treatment routine, but that didn't provide lasting relief. I later found out that I had a stress fracture in my foot. Still wanting to finish the season, I decided to continue playing despite how my foot felt. I was constantly getting treatment just to make practice and games bearable. Even so, I was hitting a stride in which my personal performance had made a great leap. Yet all these efforts sadly fell short: We won 21 games, but we didn't win the Big 12 title, and we suffered another second-round loss in the NCAA Tournament.

Finally, the 2021-22 season and my senior year arrived. It was time to make a statement and leave a lasting impression on one of the best programs in the nation. After undergoing surgery on my foot, I spent all summer working

Beating Kansas State by 19 in Allen Fieldhouse got our whole team juiced!

to get back to full health and being ready for the season. I did therapy, conditioning and drills six days a week just to get back in time for the start of the season.

We were certainly on people's radar when preseason began. The Big 12 coaches voted Remy Martin, Ochai Agbaji and me to the Preseason Big 12 First Team. In fact, they voted Remy as Preseason Player of the Year. The coaches voted KU the preseason favorite to win the league, and the Associate Press ranked us No. 3 in the country in its preseason poll. We opened well against Michigan State, but after that it became apparent that things weren't going the way we had dreamed. We were winning, but it felt like an uphill battle. Not just personally, but as a unit, we weren't playing great and it caught up to us in a buzzer-beating loss to Dayton in Florida.

During this time, I was questioning what was going on and what I needed to do to help turn it around. I was still receiving treatment almost every day, showing up to practice two hours early to receive that day's treatment and staying to receive post-practice treatment. Coach Q (Fred Quartlebaum), our director of basketball operations, is a man who is big on culture, and he constantly reminded us that we had a culture to uphold. That's exactly what we did as a team. It wasn't until the St. John's game in early December that I saw a glimpse of my old self. It was definitely due to the reassurance of our culture.

At the start of conference play we played some major nail-biters. We went to overtime against Texas Tech in the Fieldhouse, and Ochai (Agbaji) hit a dagger late to send us into another overtime. We won in the second overtime, and Ochai had 37 points. The Iowa State game at home was another hard-fought game that came down to one possession. This time Dajuan hit the game-winning layup to win it.

Our confidence was high entering our Big 12/SEC Challenge game against Kentucky. ESPN College GameDay in Allen Fieldhouse pumped up the crowd. But Kentucky schooled us. I can say now, though, that was the game that dictated the rest of the season. We collectively hated that feeling and vowed that we wouldn't have that feeling again. In the process of all of this, my teammates and I were receiving backlash from not only critics, but also our own fan base. But we as a team focused only on what we could control and continued to lift each other up.

Texas Tech is always tough, so we were happy to beat them in Kansas City and take home the Big 12 Championship trophy.

We kept moving forward through conference play embracing all the ups and downs that came with each practice and game. Preparation was vital at this point in the season. Scouting reports could make or break a game. Then came the most nerve-racking game I've played in since my first game in the Fieldhouse: Senior Night against Texas with the Big 12 regular-season title on the line. I knew that all the preparation in practice and the weight room, and all the training, had equipped me for this moment. I felt I was capable of letting loose and playing freely. After a very tense game the crowd's cheers reinforced that the Big 12 championship was, in fact, back in Lawrence.

Even after that great feeling and celebration, our entire team knew there was more to be done. Before the Big 12 tournament championship game against Texas Tech, we reminded each other of what we accomplished during the regular season and how we did it. Lo and behold, the very outcome we had worked for, happened. Twice now, what felt like a personal victory was truly a team victory, because together we were able to silence the doubters when a big game was on the line.

The next day was Selection Sunday. We were ecstatic to hear that we were the top seed in the Midwest Region in the NCAA Tournament. It was now time to avenge the 2020 team that, because of Covid-19, never had this opportunity. We won the first two games in Fort Worth, and for Ochai and I, both seniors, this was the first time we'd made it out of the first weekend. We regrouped during the week and traveled to Chicago to face our next opponents in the Midwest Regional.

After beating a tough Providence team to become the winningest program of all time, we played a sluggish first half against Miami in the Elite Eight. Once again, my teammates and I blocked out the noise and played the most dominant second half of the tournament. We outscored them 47-15 to punch our ticket to the Final Four in New Orleans.

Being in New Orleans was one of the most exhilarating feelings of my life. At the same time, though, we felt slightly nervous. But I'll never forget what Coach Self told us: "You've already done all the hard work. Your reward is being here. Now just have fun." When I heard those words I honestly felt like a weight was lifted off my shoulders. The Villanova game kind of spoke for itself. My coaches and teammates continued to believe in me, so I was able to play freely. My body was feeling especially good from the great treatment I received from Ched (trainer Billy Cowgill) and Sammy Thomas, an assistant in the sports medicine department.

After that game and throughout the next day I spent most of my time and preparation making sure my body

This dunk was part of our great second half against Miami. After that, we were Final Four-bound!

felt great for the biggest game in college basketball. It was game day, and now it was time to perform. As we lined up for the jump ball, I was honestly more relaxed than I had felt for a game in a while. Ochai and I actually joked that it didn't even feel like a championship game. A lot of folks talk about my last two baskets toward the end of that game. Honestly, those two baskets were a product of my being in the zone. I was so determined and focused on making those happen that I wasn't going to let anything get in my way. I'm not sure I can hold a candle to Wilt Chamberlain or Danny Manning, but what I can say is, like both of those guys, I am a winner.

Just about everyone knows the outcome of the game, but what they may not know is how much it meant for some people. For Coach Self it meant a lot, considering all the adversity he faced during the season. For the players it meant all that time in the gym, weight room and boot camp was all worth it. For Ochai, it meant doing what he said he would when he came back to school. As for me, what it means is almost more than I can put into words. To play like I did made me feel that I overcame the noise of the doubters and trolls. I thank my coaches, teammates, trainers, my "team behind the scenes" and Jayhawk fans everywhere who convinced me of what I already knew...I was mentally strong and capable of doing what I knew I could all along. It truly was a "Banner Year!"

Rock Chalk forever!

David McCormack

This fist pump followed some of the biggest moments of my Kansas career and signaled that our title dreams were mere seconds away from being fulfilled.

I'll always remember the feeling I had helping our team win the National Championship with two buckets in the last minute-and-a-half.

2021-22 Season Averages

		FG%	3PT%	FT%	REB	AST	STL	BLK	PTS
30	**Ochai Agbaji**	47.5%	40.9%	74.3%	5.1	1.6	0.9	0.6	18.8
2	**Christian Braun**	49.5%	38.6%	73.3%	6.5	2.8	1.0	0.8	14.1
10	**Jalen Wilson**	46.1%	26.3%	72.2%	7.4	1.8	0.9	0.4	11.1
33	**David McCormack**	50.8%	0.0%	75.6%	7.0	0.9	0.6	0.8	10.6
11	**Remy Martin**	46.2%	38.2%	75.4%	3.0	2.5	0.6	0.1	8.6
3	**Dajuan Harris Jr.**	42.7%	32.3%	79.2%	1.4	4.2	1.4	0.3	5.4
44	**Mitch Lightfoot**	66.1%	50.0%	52.3%	2.8	0.4	0.3	0.8	4.6
55	**Jalen Coleman-Lands**	46.8%	44.8%	75.0%	0.7	0.3	0.2	0.1	3.7
1	**Joseph Yesufu**	33.8%	26.2%	70.0%	0.9	1.0	0.3	0.0	2.1
21	**Zach Clemence**	37.5%	27.3%	48.3%	1.8	0.4	0.3	0.3	2.1
0	**Bobby Pettiford**	53.3%	0.0%	75.0%	0.9	0.9	0.2	0.0	1.4
24	**KJ Adams Jr.**	52.0%	0.0%	60.0%	0.8	0.3	0.1	0.2	1.0
12	**Chris Teahan**	33.3%	30.0%	0-0	0.2	0.1	0.0	0.0	0.7
20	**Michael Jankovich**	28.6%	28.6%	0-0	0.2	0.0	0.0	0.0	0.6

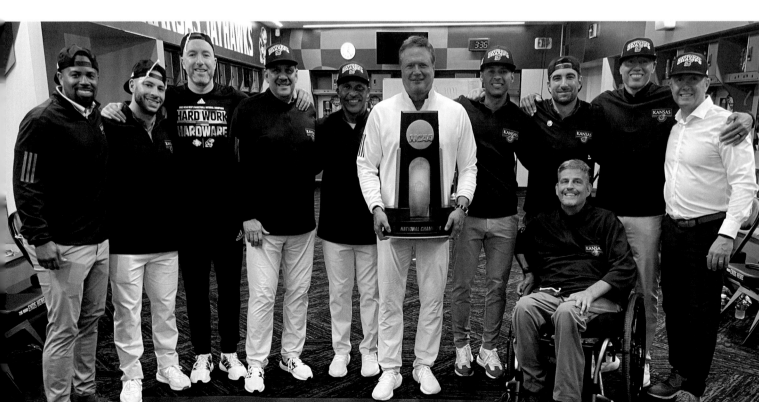

Contributors

Brian Hanni is a sportscaster and writer in Lawrence, KS., where he broadcasts radio play-by-play of athletics events for his alma mater, the University of Kansas. In his sixth season as the "Voice of the Jayhawks," Hanni had the privilege of calling KU's 2022 National Championship run; his annual poetic season recap was the initial inspiration for this book.

Banner Year is Hanni's second book. It follows *Game Maker*, a children's book that delivers the inspiring true story of James Naismith as an ambitious and creative child who grew into the inventor of Basketball. While Hanni's first love will always be behind the mic, he's enjoyed crossing over into the written word as his story-telling style evolves.

Bill Self is one of the most accomplished coaches in the history of college basketball. A first-ballot inductee into the Naismith Memorial Basketball Hall of Fame, he has led Kansas to two NCAA National Championships, nine Elite Eights and four Final Fours.

He has led Kansas to 16 Big 12 Conference regular-season titles, including an NCAA-record 14-straight between 2005 and 2018.

David McCormack is a two-time All-Big 12 selection who earned all-tournament honors at the Final Four and at the NCAA Midwest Regional. McCormack played in 132 games at KU, starting in 96 of them. He ended his career 46th on KU's all-time scoring list with 1,145 career points. He finished 19th on the KU career rebound list with 681.

McCormack is the 2022 Big 12 Scholar-Athlete of the Year (for all sports) and a three-time Academic All-Big 12 First Team honoree. He graduated from Kansas in three years with a Communications Studies degree in May 2021 and is near completion of his master's degree in digital content strategy.

Jim Marchiony retired in August 2019 after a 43-year career in college athletics, the last 16 as Associate Athletics Director at the University of Kansas. Marchiony worked for over 17 years at the NCAA, the last five years as media coordinator for the NCAA Men's Basketball Championship. He also served as a media liaison for the U.S. Olympic Committee at the 1984 Olympics in Los Angeles. He and his wife, Mary Beth, live in Dallas, where they spend much of their time spoiling their three young grandkids.

Missy Minear is a 2018 graduate of KU's William Allen White School of Journalism. The 2021-22 season was her first year as Manager of Photography at Kansas Athletics, and she had this to say about her experience: "I am grateful to the team and the staff for welcoming me and for making it so memorable. I'd also like to give a huge shout-out to my student photographers, Aiden Droge and Chad Cushing, for their outstanding photography."

(opposite page) The men's basketball staff poses with three key members of the athletics department: Deputy Athletics Director and Men's Basketball Administrator Sean Lester (right); Assistant Athletics Director, Academic and Career Counseling Vince McKamie (left); and Director of Peak Performance and Leadership Scott Ward (front right).

Head Coach Bill Self, his wife Cindy and their granddaughter Phoebe enjoy the ride down Massachusetts Street in the same 1959 powder blue Corvette that Self rode in during KU's 2008 championship parade. Then-Head Coach Larry Brown rode in the same car in the Jayhawks' 1988 championship parade.

David McCormack (left) and Ochai Agbaji get a ride and a police escort while showing off the Jayhawks' NCAA Championship trophy during KU's championship parade through downtown Lawrence.

Tens of thousands of Kansas fans packed Massachusetts Street in downtown Lawrence to celebrate with their Jayhawks during the championship parade on April 10.

The 2022 NCAA Champions Celebrate a Banner Year